The Little Science Encyclopedia

Angela Wilkes

KING*f*ISHER

NEW YORK

Project Editor Aimee Blythe
Project Designer Kelly Flynn

Editor Jenny Vaughn
Proofreader Jane Birch

Art Editors Val Wright, David Noon
Photography Tim Ridley, Nick Goodall
Prop Organizer Sarah Wilson
DTP Operator Primrose Burton

Picture Research Jane Lambert

Artwork Archivist Wendy Allison
Assistant Artwork Archivist Steve Robinson
Art Reference Isobel Balakrishnan

Production Managers Sue Wilmot, Oonagh Phelan

Cover Design Mark Bristow

Writers Chris Oxlade, Anita Ganeri

Specialist Consultants John and Sue Becklake
General Consultant Tom Schiele

KINGFISHER
Larousse Kingfisher Chambers Inc.
80 Maiden Lane
New York, New York 10038
www.kingfisherpub.com

First published as *First Encyclopedia of Science* by Kingfisher Publications Plc 1997
This edition printed in 2001

2 4 6 8 10 9 7 5 3 1

1TR/0601/SF/MAR/157MA

LIBRARY OF CONGRESS CATALOGING-IN-PUBLICATION DATA
has been applied for.

ISBN 0-7534-5402-5

Printed in China

Your book

Your *Little Science Encyclopedia* tells you all about the world around you. It explains how things work and why things happen. It is packed with pictures to help you learn. There are also lots of experiments for you to try. These will help you find out more about science and about being a scientist.

◁ There is information about each picture printed next to it. Look at the arrows to help you see which information goes with which picture.

▷ Step-by-step instructions show you how to do the experiments.

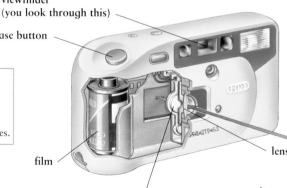

1   2   3

viewfinder
(you look through this)

shutter release button

◁ Some pictures show things that have many different parts, such as this camera. Labels show you what each part is called.

Fact box
• These boxes contain extra information, facts, and figures.

film

lens

shutter

◁ This little person is telling you to move on to the next page.

This sign means
DANGER!
TAKE CARE!

Find out more
If you want to find out more about each topic, look at this box. It will tell you which pages to look at.

Contents

Acid

Acids are chemicals. Many fruits contain acids. Vinegar and lemon juice are acids, too. These are weak acids. They make things taste sour.

Some acids are strong and can eat away at things. They are dangerous because they burn. But they can be useful. For example, some strong acids are used in making plastics. You have strong acids in your stomach to help you digest your food.

△ 1 You can find out if a substance is an acid. Ask an adult to chop some red cabbage and put it into hot water. Let it cool, then pour the liquid into clean glasses.

▷ Lemons contain an acid called citric acid. This gives the lemon its sharp taste.

 Strong acids can burn. They are dangerous.

△ 2 To test a substance, mix it with some of the cabbage water. Acids turn the cabbage water red. What happens when you test lemon juice? Now try baking soda. This is an alkali, which means it is the opposite of an acid. Alkalis turn the cabbage water green.

◁ These trees have been killed by acid rain. Acid rain forms when gases made by burning fuels, such as coal, mix with drops of water in the air. This makes a weak acid, which harms plants and eats away rocks and buildings.

Find out more
Air and Atmosphere
Chemistry and Chemicals
Fuels

Air and Atmosphere

You cannot see air, but you can feel it when the wind blows. Air is a mixture of different gases. The main ones are nitrogen and oxygen. There is a blanket of air all around the Earth, called the atmosphere.

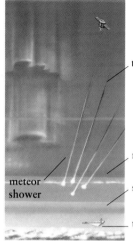

thermosphere

mesosphere

meteor shower

stratosphere

troposphere

△ The air in the atmosphere gets thinner the farther it gets from the Earth's surface. Each layer has a name.

▽ When we breathe, we take in air. Our bodies need the oxygen in the air to stay alive. We breathe out carbon dioxide as waste. Plants take in carbon dioxide, which they need to make food. They give out oxygen as waste.

△▷ This experiment shows that air has weight. The items you will need are shown above. Tape a balloon to each end of a stick. Lay a pencil between two cans and balance the stick across it. Mark the stick where it crosses the pencil. Now blow up one of the balloons. Tape it back in place, making sure that the mark on the stick is still over the pencil. Do you know why the stick doesn't balance?

Fact box
• A layer of ozone gas in the atmosphere protects living things from the Sun's harmful rays.
• The air in a bedroom weighs about the same as you do.

Find out more
Earth
Gases
Living things
Weather

Atoms

Everything that exists is made up of atoms. Atoms are so small that they are impossible to see without a special machine. Some things are made of just one kind of atom. For example, gold is made of gold atoms. Iron is made of iron atoms. But most things are made of several different kinds of atoms joined together in groups called molecules.

Fact box
• There are about 100 million atoms in a speck of dust.
• Scientists have found over 100 different kinds of atom.

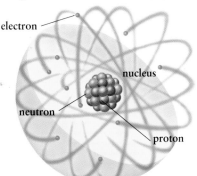

electron

nucleus

neutron

proton

△ It is very difficult to break apart the nucleus (central part) of an atom. When a nucleus does split, it releases a huge amount of energy, which can then cause a nuclear explosion.

◁ The middle part of an atom is the nucleus. It is made of particles (pieces), called protons and neutrons. Particles called electrons move around the nucleus.

Find out more
Chemistry and Chemicals
Gases
Liquids
Nuclear energy
Solids

△ These children are acting the part of an oxygen molecule. It is made of two oxygen atoms joined together.

△ A molecule of water is made of one oxygen atom joined to two hydrogen atoms.

Battery

A battery is a source of electricity. The electricity is made inside the battery by chemicals. When you turn on a flashlight, electricity flows along a wire from one end of the battery, through a bulb, and back to the battery to make the flashlight glow. After a while, the chemicals are used up and can't produce any more electricity. Then we say that the battery is flat.

△ All the machines above use batteries to work. Because the batteries inside them are small, the machines are light and portable. This makes them easy to carry around.

▽ This battery is rechargeable. This means that when it runs down the chemicals can be replaced by sending electricity through it. Most cars have battery like this to start their engines.

chemical paste

△ This type of battery is used in a flashlight or a radio. It is called a dry battery, because the chemicals inside it are like a dry paste.

Never play with batteries or take them apart. They can be dangerous.

▷ This car has an electric motor instead of a gasoline engine. The electricity for the motor comes from rechargeable batteries inside the car.

Find out more

Chemistry and Chemicals
Electricity

Biology

How does your body work? Why are leaves green? Biology is the study of living things, so it can help answer questions like these. It tells us how animals and plants live, grow, produce young, and find food.

   Doctors use biology to find out about disease and medicines. Scientists who study biology are called biologists.

a stem, magnified eight times

△ Biologists often use a microscope to study tiny objects, such as the cells inside plant stems. Try looking at animal hairs or a leaf under a microscope.

▽ Biologists often choose to study just one kind of living thing. Some biologists study mostly plants, others study mostly animals. They may make trips to other parts of the world, like this tropical rain forest, to study the plants or animals that live there.

△ Like other scientists, biologists often work in laboratories. This biologist is studying some specially grown seedlings.

Find out more
Experiment
Human body
Living things
Medicine
Z (for Zoology)

Calculator

A calculator is a machine that adds, subtracts, multiplies, and divides. We often use electronic calculators. These can help us to work out problems with lots of numbers quickly and without making mistakes.

▽ This calculator is called an abacus. The different beads stand for different numbers. You work out the problems by sliding the beads along the wires. Calculators like this have been used for over 5,000 years.

▽ The display window on a calculator shows each stage of a calculation while you are doing it. When you have finished the calculation, the answer appears in the window.

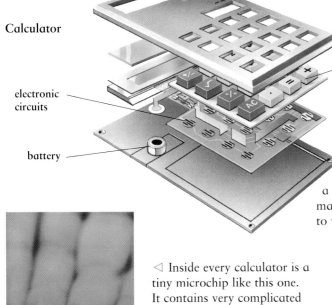

display window

Calculator

electronic circuits

battery

keypad

◁ You press the buttons on the keypad to enter the problem into the calculator.

◁ This calculator has a small battery inside it that makes the electricity it needs to work.

◁ Inside every calculator is a tiny microchip like this one. It contains very complicated electrical circuits. When electricity passes through these, they do the calculations.

Find out more
Battery
Computers
Electricity
Mathematics
Numbers

Camera

A camera is a machine for taking photographs. When you take a photograph of an object, light bounces off it and in through the camera's lens to hit the film inside. The light changes chemicals in the film. When the film is processed (treated with more chemicals), pictures appear.

▽ **3** Point your camera at a window or a light so that light streams through the pinhole. Can you see an upside-down image on the tracing paper? You will see the image better if you cut out stray light by putting a towel over your head like the boy in the picture above.

1

△ **1** Try making this simple camera, which is called a pinhole camera. You need a small box. Cut off its ends and color the inside with a black marker.

2

△ **2** Cover one end with tracing paper. Cover the other end with brown paper and pierce a small hole in its center.

3

film

Camera

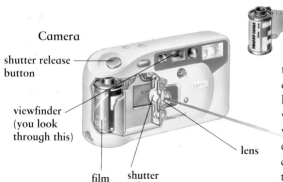

shutter release button

viewfinder (you look through this)

lens

film   shutter

◁ Here you can see the parts of a compact camera. Behind the lens there is a shutter, which opens and shuts very fast. It lets just enough light into the camera for a picture to form on the film.

Find out more
Chemistry and Chemicals
Color
Light and Lenses

Chemistry and Chemicals

Chemistry is the study of what things are made from. People who study chemistry are called chemists. Chemicals are the solids, liquids, and gases that chemists use or make.

Different chemicals are useful in different ways. We use some for cleaning and others for cooking. Some are used in factories, to make plastics or paint. Farmers use chemicals to help crops to grow, and to kill weeds or insects.

carbon atom

hydrogen atom

△ Like all substances, chemicals are made up of atoms. These cling together in groups called molecules. This picture shows a model of a polyethylene molecule. It is made up of carbon and hydrogen atoms.

▷ Some chemicals seem to disappear when you put them in water. We say they dissolve. How well do salt, sugar, and flour dissolve?

sugar

salt

flour

sugar

oil

▽ Some chemicals look the same, but you can tell them apart by feeling them. Try touching lemon juice and cooking oil.

Don't touch any chemicals unless an adult says they are safe. Some are poisonous. Some can burn your skin.

salt

△ Sugar and salt are chemicals that look the same. Is it easy to tell them apart by tasting them?

lemon juice

∇ Rust is made when the metal iron combines with the gas oxygen (which is in the air). When chemicals join together to make new chemicals, we call it a chemical reaction.

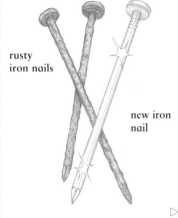

rusty iron nails

new iron nail

△ Hundreds of years ago, people called alchemists tried to make gold from other kinds of metals. This was impossible, but, as they worked, alchemists learned about what happened when they mixed different chemicals. You could say that alchemists were the first chemists.

▷ We can tell some chemicals by their smell. Slices of potato and apple look the same, but smell different.

potato

pebble

polystyrene pebble

apple

Fact box

• Chemicals can occur in very different forms. For example, graphite (found in pencils) and diamonds are both forms of the chemical carbon.

△ We can tell some chemicals apart by their weight. For example, a lump of polystyrene weighs much less than a rock of the same size.

Find out more

Acid
Atoms
Fuels
Gases
Liquids
Solids

Clocks

We use clocks to measure time. Inside every clock there is a special part that works at the same, regular speed. In electric clocks it is a regular electrical signal. This controls the speed at which the hands move, or how often the numbers on the display change. Some older clocks have a swinging pendulum to move the hands at a regular speed.

△ Clocks come in all shapes and sizes. Many are battery-powered. Some watches are "digital." This means the time is shown as numbers in a window. Other watches have a dial and hands.

swing   swing

△ A pendulum is a weight on the end of a string or rod. Each swing of the pendulum takes exactly the same time.

tweezers

cogs

▷ Inside this watch there is a spring that is wound up very tightly. As it unwinds, it moves tiny wheels called cogs, and these move the hands. The wheels, springs, and cogs are so small that watchmakers have to use fine tweezers to mend or move them.

◁ This old-fashioned grandfather clock has a long pendulum to control the speed of its hands.

◁ Long ago, people used sundials instead of clocks. The dial is marked in hours. The Sun shines on the pointer, which casts a shadow. This shows you the time.

Find out more
Day and Night
Energy
Machines

Color

When we see color, we see colored light. Ordinary light, such as sunlight, is called white light. It seems to have no color, but it is really a mixture of every color there is.

When we see an object, what we actually see is light bouncing off it into our eyes. Often, only a few of the colors in the light bounce off the object. A leaf looks green, for example, because only green light bounces off it.

Fact box
• The pictures in this book are made up of tiny colored dots. The colors are yellow, a kind of dark pink, a shade of blue, and black. These four colors mix together to make all the colors you see.

1

△ **1** Put a saucer on a sheet of stiff white card. Draw around it and cut out the circle.

2

△ **2** Draw lines to divide the circle into three. Color one part red, one part green, and one part blue.

3

△ **3** Push a pencil through the center of the circle. Spin it like a top. The three colors mix together, making the disk look white.

△ A rainbow happens when the Sun shines during a shower of rain. The light reflects (bounces off) the raindrops and the light breaks up into all its different colors.

▽ Red, blue, and green are called the primary colors of light because they mix together to make white light.

△ Flowers are often brightly colored. Their colors signal to insects and birds that inside there is sweet nectar, which they like to drink. This hummingbird uses its long, thin beak to reach deep inside the flower.

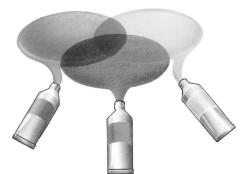

▽ The ladybug's coloring warns other animals that it is not good to eat.

△ Red, blue, and yellow are the primary colors of paint. With these three colors you can make any color you want.

▷ We use colored lights to send messages. On traffic lights, red means "stop," yellow means "take care," and green means "go."

◁ This insect is exactly the same color as the leaves it lives on. Its disguise makes it difficult for its enemies to see, and protects the insect from being eaten.

Find out more

Light and Lenses
Living things

Computers

A computer is an amazing machine. It can do calculations, store and find information. It works using microchips (very small electrical circuits) that act as its brain and memory. A computer cannot think for itself. A human being has to give it a set of instructions, called a program. These are usually stored on a disk inside the computer.

△ A CD-ROM is a disk containing information that the computer can turn into words, pictures, and sounds.

▷ The letters and pictures that appear on a computer screen are made of tiny dots of colored light called pixels. This archaeopteryx shows how pixels make up a picture.

pixels

◁ You move a mouse around to point at things on the screen. A cursor on the screen follows your movements.

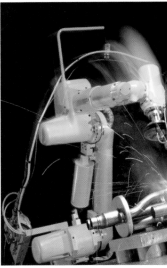

△ This is a robot that puts car parts together in a factory. It is controlled by a computer that has been programmed to tell the robot what to do.

Fact box
• The world's most powerful computers can do more than a billion calculations in a second.

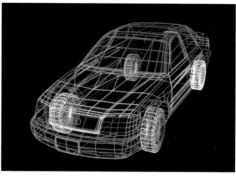

△ Engineers use computers to design cars. The picture on the screen shows what the car will look like when it is built.

bar code

bar code reader

laser beam

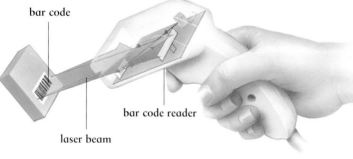

◁ Bar codes are patterns of black and white stripes. They contain coded information about the objects they are printed on. A laser beam scans the bar code and sends the information to a computer. You can see an example of this in a supermarket.

◁ With a headset like this you can have the feeling of being in another world—perhaps among the dinosaurs, or in Ancient Rome. This is called virtual reality. The headset shows pictures of the world created by the computer. It also plays sounds made by the people and animals in that world.

Find out more
Calculator
Electricity
Mathematics
Numbers
Technology

Day and Night

Days and nights happen because the Earth spins as it travels around the Sun. The Sun shines onto the side of the Earth facing it. As the Earth spins, different parts of the Earth's surface get more or less sunlight. When the part of the Earth you live on is in the sunlight, you have day.

◁ Most people sleep at night and play or work in the day. But some animals, such as owls, sleep by day and look for food at night. They are called nocturnal.

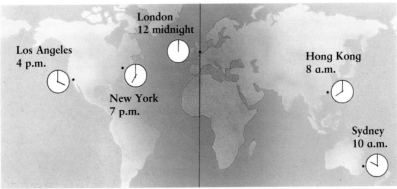

London
12 midnight

Los Angeles
4 p.m.

New York
7 p.m.

Hong Kong
8 a.m.

Sydney
10 a.m.

△ When it is day where you are, it is night on the other side of the world. The time changes as you travel around the world.

◁ Try this experiment to see how day and night happen. Work with a friend in a dark room. Shine a torch on one side of a globe. The other person turns the globe around slowly. Can you see how each part of the globe is in the light for a time, while the rest is in shadow?

Find out more
Clocks
Earth
Living things
Seasons
Solar System

Earth

The Earth is the planet we live on. It formed about 4.5 billion years ago from a cloud of dust, rock, and gas. Since then, volcanoes, earthquakes, wind, and rain have changed its surface. Scientists think the Earth is the only planet in the Solar System where plants and animals can live.

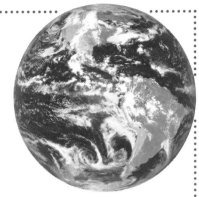

△ Two-thirds of the Earth is covered in salty seawater. Around the Earth is a blanket of air, called the atmosphere.

▽ The Earth is a giant ball of rock. Beneath the surface, this rock is so hot that some of it is molten (melted) and runny. Around the outside, the rock forms a hard crust.

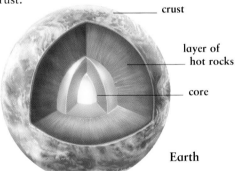

crust

layer of hot rocks

core

Earth

▷ Millions of years ago, the land on Earth was joined together in one huge continent. Gradually, it split up and formed the continents we have today. These are still moving slowly. Millions of years from now, the surface of the Earth will look very different from the way it does now.

▽ The Earth's crust is made up of enormous sections called plates. These move very, very slowly. Sometimes they push against each other and crumple. When this happens, mountains form.

Fact box
• People once thought that the Earth was flat and you could fall off the edge.

Find out more
Air and Atmosphere
Day and Night
Solar System
Volcano
Water
Weather

Electricity

Electricity is a form of energy. It is also known as electrical energy. We get some electricity from batteries, but most of the electricity in our homes is made in power plants. It reaches our homes along thick cables. The electricity flows along these, like a current in a stream. This is why we call it current electricity. Electricity that does not flow in a current is called static electricity.

△ A flash of lightning is a huge spark of electricity. Static electricity forms in clouds and jumps through the air. It may travel from cloud to cloud, or down to the ground.

▽ Run a plastic comb through your hair quickly, several times. Hold the comb over some bits of paper and see how it attracts the paper. Combing your hair made static electricity form on the comb. Static electricity on an object can make it attract other objects.

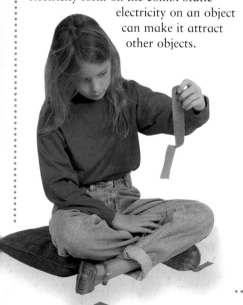

△ Electricity only flows along wires if they are joined in a loop called a circuit. In a flashlight, a circuit joins one end of a battery to the other, through a bulb and a switch. The circuit here works in the same way. The bulb will only light up if there is no gap anywhere in the circuit.

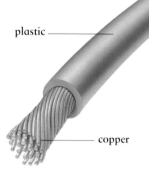

plastic

copper

◁ Some materials will allow electricity to flow through them. We call these conductors. Most electrical wires are made from copper, which is a good conductor. These wires are covered in plastic to insulate them. This means that if the wire touches another conductor, the electricity will not flow out into it.

Electricity is dangerous. Never play with electrical sockets or electrical machines.

▷ **1** Try an experiment to see which materials are conductors and which are not. (Materials that do not let electricity through are called insulators.) This picture shows everything you need for this experiment. Start by making a circuit, like the one on the opposite page.

1

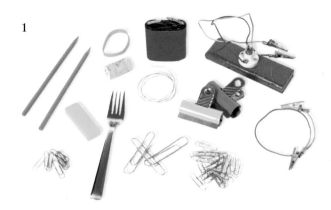

2

△ **2** Try making a gap in the circuit. What happens to the bulb? Fix a paperclip so that it closes the gap. What happens?

3

△ **3** Now try putting other objects in the gap, such as a fork or a rubber band. Which ones are good conductors? Which are insulators?

▷ These tall towers hold up thick electrical wires, or cables. These carry electricity from generating stations to towns and cities. When it gets there, it travels along cables buried under the ground.

◁ These model cars are controlled by changing the amount of electricity flowing in the metal racetrack. In many machines, the flow of electricity is controlled using electronics, which are very tiny but complicated circuits.

▽ There is an electric motor in this model train. Electricity flows along the metal tracks and into the train. It makes the motor spin, and this moves the wheels of the train. When the electricity stops, the train stops.

Find out more

Battery
Calculator
Computers
Energy
Magnets

Energy

Nothing can happen without energy. Energy is what makes everything work, including you. There are many different types of energy. There is movement energy, light energy, heat energy, chemical energy, and electrical energy. Energy can change from one type to another, but it cannot be made from scratch or destroyed.

△ This is New York. In a big city like this, huge amounts of energy are needed to heat, light, and give power to offices and homes, and to make buses, cars, and trains run.

△ Sound is a type of energy. Beating the drum makes a sound which travels through the air in waves. When the waves reach your ears, you hear the sound.

▽ Plants use energy from sunshine to make food for themselves. All living things, including plants and animals, need energy from food to stay alive. Some animals eat plants, some eat other animals, and some eat both. In the end, all plants and animals get the energy they need from the Sun.

energy from the Sun

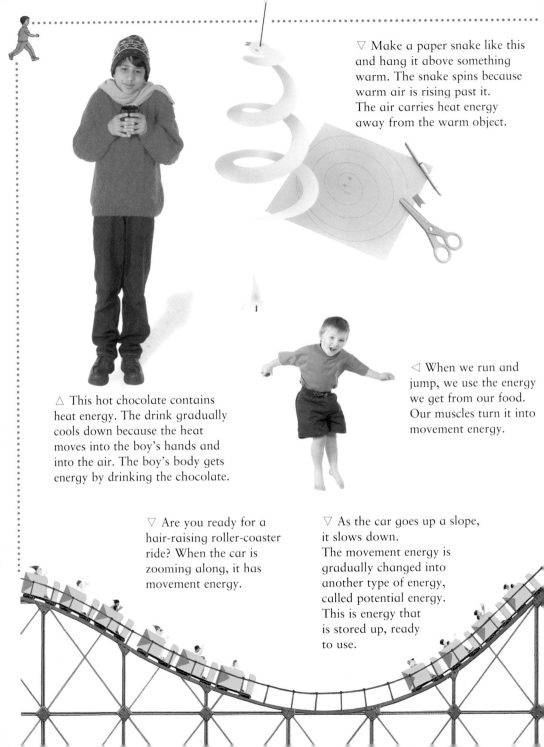

▽ Make a paper snake like this and hang it above something warm. The snake spins because warm air is rising past it. The air carries heat energy away from the warm object.

△ This hot chocolate contains heat energy. The drink gradually cools down because the heat moves into the boy's hands and into the air. The boy's body gets energy by drinking the chocolate.

◁ When we run and jump, we use the energy we get from our food. Our muscles turn it into movement energy.

▽ Are you ready for a hair-raising roller-coaster ride? When the car is zooming along, it has movement energy.

▽ As the car goes up a slope, it slows down. The movement energy is gradually changed into another type of energy, called potential energy. This is energy that is stored up, ready to use.

▽ Wind is air with movement energy. The blades of these wind turbines catch the movement energy from the air, and the turbines turn it into electrical energy.

△ Deep under the Earth's crust, the rock is very hot. In some places, there is hot rock near the surface, too. The heat energy in the rock can be very useful. Water is pumped through the rock, so it gets hot. Then it is piped into homes. This kind of energy is called geothermal energy.

▷ For thousands of years, people have used the heat energy and light energy from fire. We still use it to cook food and keep us warm.

△ As you hurtle down the slope again, you soon gather speed. The potential energy is changing back into movement energy.

Fact box

• You could run 6,500 feet on the energy you get from eating a chocolate bar— but only 160 feet on the energy you get from eating a lettuce leaf.

ancient forest

◁ We get a lot of energy from burning coal, oil, and gas. These lie under the ground or under the seabed. They formed millions of years ago from the remains of plants and animals. Ancient remains of plants and animals are called fossils, so the fuels are called fossil fuels.

coal—the remains of an ancient forest

1

2

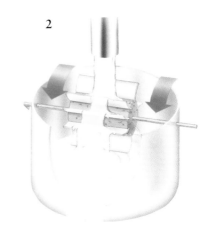

△ **1** You can use the energy in falling water to turn a waterwheel. Ask an adult to cut slots in a cork and rectangles from a plastic bottle. Slide the rectangles into the slots to make paddles.

◁ **2** Push two pieces of stiff wire into the cork, one at each end, as the picture shows. (Ask an adult to help you.) Hold the wheel under a faucet and run the water over it. The wheel spins. This movement energy can be used to power machines or make electricity.

▷ There is a special kind of waterwheel, called a turbine, inside this dam. Water flows from behind the dam and makes the turbine turn. This turns a machine called a generator, which changes the movement energy into electrical energy.

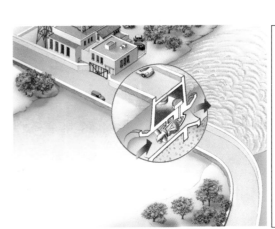

Find out more

Electricity
Engines
Force
Fuels
Hot and Cold
Machines
Melting and
Boiling
Nuclear energy
Waves

Engines

Many machines have engines to make them work. For example, a car has an engine which makes its wheels turn. A ship has an engine that turns propellers in the water. A jet aircraft's engines push it through the air. All these engines needs fuel to work. The engine turns the energy in the fuel into movement energy.

△ A rocket engine makes a stream of hot gas. The stream rushes out of the base of the rocket. It pushes the rocket upwards.

Fact box

• The power of an engine is measured in units called horsepower. This word was invented by the first engineers, who compared engine power to horse power.

Gasoline engine

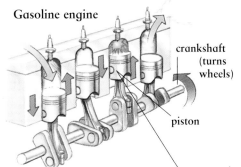

crankshaft (turns wheels)

piston

△ Inside a car engine are pistons that move up and down in cylinders. A mixture of gasoline and air is sucked into the cylinder. The mixture explodes when the spark plug makes a spark, pushing the piston down. The cylinders move down one after the other, turning the crankshaft.

Close-up of a piston

spark plug (makes the spark)

explosion

piston

steam locomotive

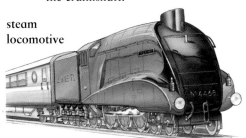

◁ This old locomotive had a steam engine. Fire in the engine boiled water to make steam. This pushed pistons in and out, turning the wheels.

Find out more
Energy
Fire
Flight
Fuels
Machines
Space travel
Water

Environment

Your environment is where you live. It is your home, your school, and all the people, animals, and plants around you. It includes the air above you, the weather, and the soil beneath your feet. Like you, all living things have their own environment. It may be the same as yours, or it may be quite different, such as under the sea, or high in the mountains.

△ An environment can be damaged or even destroyed. For example, when people cut down forests, animals may die because they have nowhere to live and nothing to eat.

▽ A coral reef is one of many environments in the sea. Thousands of plants, fish, and other sea creatures live among the coral.

△ Some animals are well suited to their environment. This goat lives high in the mountains. It is a good climber and can leap from rock to rock.

Find out more
Earth
Seasons
Weather

Experiment

Scientists are always trying to find out more about the world we live in. They try out their ideas using tests, called experiments. Some experiments are very quick and easy to do. Others are very long and complicated. Some do not work well the first time and have to be done again. Here is an experiment you can do: a test to see which ball bounces highest.

△ **1** You will need different kinds of balls, such as a tennis ball and a soft sponge ball, and paper and pencil to record the information. You also need to make a long measuring stick and mark it in feet or meters.

▷ **4** Study your results. What do they show? Before you did the experiment, did you guess how high each ball would bounce? Were you right?

◁ **2** Get a friend to hold the measure straight. Now drop each ball from the same height. Before you drop a ball, try guessing how high it will bounce.

Find out more

Biology
Chemistry and Chemicals
Energy
Physics

△ **3** Note the type of ball and how high it bounces. Write this down and compare the results.

Fire

For millions of years, people have used fire to cook their food and to keep themselves warm.

Fire happens when a chemical combines with oxygen (one of the gases that makes up air). As this happens, heat and light are given off, and you can often see flames. Some materials, such as wood, burn well. Others, such as rock, don't burn at all.

△ When you strike a match, the friction makes enough heat for the chemicals on the tip of the matchstick to catch fire.

Fire is dangerous. Never play with matches or go near fires. Never play with fireworks.

△ Firefighters use water to cool a fire and put it out. Sometimes they use foam. This stops oxygen from reaching the fire, and the burning stops. Firefighters wear special clothes to protect them from flames and smoke.

▽ Firework rockets like these contain explosives. They burn very fast and send out hot gases which shoot the rocket into the sky.

Find out more

Chemistry and Chemicals
Energy
Engines
Fuels

Flight

Things that fly need an upward push, or force, to keep them in the air. This force is called lift. Without lift, another force, called gravity, pulls them back toward the ground. Aircraft, birds, and insects all have wings. As they fly along, their wings use the air to make lift.

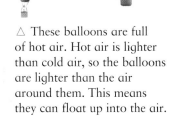

△ These balloons are full of hot air. Hot air is lighter than cold air, so the balloons are lighter than the air around them. This means they can float up into the air.

▷ Birds have strong muscles which make their wings flap up and down. Some birds, such as this seabird, have long, thin wings. They use them to glide as well as flap.

△ Some small aircraft have a propeller at the front. This is like a fan. It spins very fast, pushing air backwards and pulling the aircraft through the air.

◁ An aircraft's wings only make lift when the aircraft is speeding through the air. The air flows over and under the wing. Because of the wing's special curved shape, this makes lift.

◁ Some seeds, such as these dandelion seeds, are very light and fluffy. They drift with the breeze until they reach a good place for growing.

△ A helicopter has a spinning rotor. The rotor makes lift even if the helicopter is hovering still in the air. Here, a helicopter is being used to rescue a person from the sea.

◁ Blow hard on a dandelion. Watch the seeds. How long is it before they reach the ground?

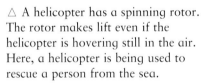

◁ Put a piece of tissue paper on your bottom lip and blow gently to make air flow across the top of the paper. The tissue paper lifts up. A wing works in the ʃme way. Its shape makes air flow ster over the top than th ꞁttom.

Find out more

Air and Atmosphere
Engines
Floating
Force
Gravity
Pressure
Space travel

Floating

Why do some things float in water, and some things sink? Think about the space something takes up. This space is called its volume.

Things float if they weigh less than the same volume of water. A beach ball floats in water because it does not weigh as much as water with the same volume. A coin weighs more than water with the same volume, so it sinks.

△ These logs are floating down the river from the forest to the lumber mill. They float well because wood is lighter than water.

▷ Test a few objects to see if they float. Then choose something that floats and try pushing it down into the water. Can you feel the water pushing it upward? This upward push is called upthrust. Upthrust is the force that makes things float.

Fact box

• It's easier to float in salty water than in freshwater. The Dead Sea, between Israel and Jordan, is so salty that you can float without having to swim.

◁ A submarine can float or sink. To make it sink, water is let into tanks in the submarine's hull. This makes it heavier. To make it float again, air is pumped into the tanks to empty the water out. This makes it lighter.

Find out more
Flight
Force
Liquids
Pressure
Water

Force

A force is a push or a pull. Forces can make things move. For example, to throw a ball, you push it hard to make it move quickly through the air. You also need a force to stop something moving. When you catch a ball, your hands push against it to slow it down. Engines and motors make forces that cause machines to move. The force of gravity pulls everything downward toward the Earth.

△ This boy is pulling on the bar. He exerts a force that lifts him up. When he lets go, the force of gravity pulls him down to the ground.

▽ The force of gravity pulls this girl down the slide. Another force, called friction, slows her down slightly. But because the surface of the slide is smooth, she hardly notices. There is more friction if surfaces are rough.

◁ Forces can squash or stretch things. When this boy jumps on his pogo stick he squashes the ball under his feet. The ball then pushes him back upward into the air.

▷ These children are both exerting the same amount of force on the rope, but the forces are pulling in opposite directions. The two forces cancel each other out, so the rope does not move and neither do the children.

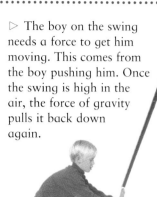

▷ The boy on the swing needs a force to get him moving. This comes from the boy pushing him. Once the swing is high in the air, the force of gravity pulls it back down again.

▷ This boy is using his leg muscles to exert force. He pushes backwards with one leg to make himself roll along on the other leg. The wheels turn smoothly, so there is little friction to slow them down.

▷ In these pictures, arrows show the direction the force is pushing or pulling. This girl is pushing as hard as she can.

△ It's much easier when two people push. The more force that is exerted on the sled, the more quickly it will speed up.

▷ Wherever there is a force working in one direction, there is also a twin force, working just as strongly, in the opposite direction. This means that when you push something, like this wall, you can feel its force matching your own.

Forces can make things stretch. Try making this weighing machine.

△ **1** Fix a large sheet of paper to a door as shown above. Put a large rubber band around the door knob. Use a strong paperclip to hang a bag on the rubber band.

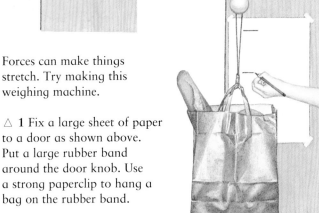

◁ **2** Mark the paper next to the bottom end of the rubber band. Now put objects in the bag. Each time you add an object, mark where the bottom end of the rubber band reaches. See how the weight of the objects stretches the rubber. How can you find out which objects are the heaviest?

◁ It is harder to push things up a hill than along a flat surface. This is because you have to push against the force of gravity.

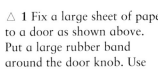

Find out more
Energy
Flight
Friction
Gravity
Motion
Pressure

Friction

Friction is a force which tries to stop one surface sliding against another. There is more friction between rough surfaces than between smooth surfaces. Friction stops your feet sliding on the ground as you walk. It stops things slipping from your grasp, and stops bicycle tires skidding when you brake. Look out for friction at home or at school.

△ Find out how different surfaces are affected by friction. Slide different objects down a slope. Try coins, pens and pencils, and an eraser. Which ones slide most easily?

Fact box

• When surfaces rub together, friction makes heat. That's why you rub your hands to warm them up.

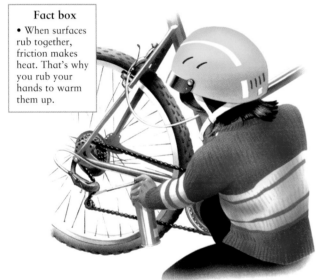

◁ This girl is putting oil on her bicycle gears and chain. The oil reduces friction. It lets the gear wheels turn more easily and makes the chain more flexible. This makes pedaling easier and stops the gears from wearing out. Oil also stops the metal parts from rusting.

◁ Friction also tries to slow things down that are moving through the air. There is less air friction on things with a smooth, streamlined shape, such as this sports car.

Find out more

Air and Atmosphere
Force
Machines
Water

Fuels

Fuels are sources of energy. We need energy for heating, cooking, lighting and to make machines work. This energy comes from fuels. When fuels burn, they release energy. Some fuels, such as coal, oil, and gas are found under the ground. Food is also a fuel. Animals eat food to get energy to live.

△ Food is fuel for your body. It provides you with the energy you need to move— or even just to sit and think.

◁ The engines in cars and other vehicles make dirty waste gases when they burn fuel. These gases float into the air making it dirty and harmful to people, other animals, and plants. This dirtiness is called pollution. Modern cars have special parts that cut down the amount of pollution they make.

▷ Power plants make electricity for our homes, offices, and factories. Most use fossil fuels—coal, oil, and gas. Every day, hundreds of tons of coal are burned at this power station. This makes heat energy, which is turned into movement energy, and then into electrical energy.

◁ Oil is often found deep under the seabed. To get it out, a deep hole has to be drilled. Then, the oil is pumped up through long pipes. Oil is used to make gasoline, diesel, and other kinds of fuel.

Find out more
Earth
Electricity
Energy
Living things
Machines
Materials
Nuclear energy

Gases

Everything that exists is a solid, a liquid, or a gas. These are called the states of matter. Gases are different from other states. They spread out to fill the space they are in. They can also be squeezed into a smaller space. You cannot squeeze a liquid or a solid.

Most gases are invisible. But some have a strong smell, so you know they are there.

△ Try making a gas and watch it fill a balloon. You need vinegar, a bottle, some bicarbonate of soda, a balloon, and a funnel.

1

2

3

△ **1** Pour some vinegar into the bottle, until it is about two inches deep. Now pour some soda into the balloon. Use the funnel for this.

△ **2** Fit the neck of the balloon over the top of the bottle. Then shake the balloon so that the soda drops into the bottle.

△ **3** The soda and the vinegar fizz and give off bubbles of carbon dioxide gas. The gas fills the bottle and blows up the balloon.

◁ The molecules, or tiny particles, that make up a gas have a lot of space between them. Gases can be squeezed into a smaller space by pushing the molecules closer together.

Find out more

Air and Atmosphere
Chemistry and Chemicals
Liquids
Solids

Gravity

Gravity is a force. It pulls everything toward the ground. When you weigh something, you are measuring how strongly gravity is pulling it. The Earth's gravity keeps your feet on the ground and stops objects from flying off into space. It also keeps the Moon in orbit around the Earth. Everything in the Universe has gravity.

△ This stilt-walker's weight is high up, so he has a high center of gravity. If he leans slightly to one side, gravity will tip him over. It takes great skill to stay standing.

▷ This clown has a wide, heavy base, but a very light top. We say it has a low center of gravity. If you push it over, gravity brings it back upright again.

◁ When this boy throws the balls into the air, gravity pulls them back down again. If there were no gravity, the balls would go on traveling upward into space.

Fact box
• The Moon's gravity pulls on the Earth and makes the water in the oceans move. This is what makes the tides rise and fall.

△ When you weigh yourself, you are measuring how much gravity is pulling you downward. The scales measure this and show your weight in pounds.

▽ **1** Do you think heavy things fall faster than lighter ones? Try this experiment to find out. You need two balls that are the same size, but different weights.

◁ **2** It is important to drop both balls at the same time, from the same height. The boy on the left is telling the girls when to let go.

▷ **3** Which ball reaches the ground first? They should both land together. This is because the weight of an object makes no difference to how fast it falls.

▽ The Moon is much smaller than the Earth, so it has less gravity. This astronaut will find that the gravity on the Moon does not pull him down nearly as hard as the gravity on Earth.

▷ You could jump much higher on the Moon because there is less gravity pulling you down. On Earth, gravity keeps pulling you strongly back to the ground.

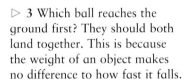

Find out more

Earth
Energy
Flight
Force
Satellites
Space travel
Universe

Hot and Cold

To make things hotter or colder you have to add or take away heat energy. Heat energy always moves from hotter places to colder places. For example, a hot drink soon cools down because heat moves from it into the cooler air around it. When we measure how hot or cold something is, we say we are measuring its temperature.

△ **1** Dip a coin in water and put it on top of a large soda bottle. Hold your hands around the bottle.

250°C
480°F

hot oven

boiling point of water

100°C
212°F

▽ When water boils, molecules of water escape into the air. These molecules form an invisible gas called water vapor. This water vapor soon cools in the air and turns into tiny drops of water called steam.

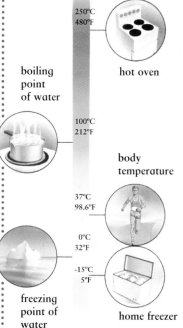

body temperature

37°C
98.6°F

0°C
32°F

-15°C
5°F

freezing point of water

home freezer

steam

water vapor

boiling water

△ **2** The coin lifts up. This is because your hands warm the colder air in the bottle. The air expands (gets bigger) when it gets hotter and this pushes the coin up.

△ We measure temperature in degrees Fahrenheit (°F) or degrees Celsius (°C). Celsius is sometimes called degrees centigrade.

◁ Thermometers are used to measure temperature. The type of thermometer shown here is used to measure the temperature of a human body.

Find out more
Energy
Fire
Flight
Gases
Melting and Boiling

Human body

Your body is like a complicated machine. Inside and out, it is made up of lots of different working parts. How many do you know? Each of these parts has a job to do. For example, you think with your brain, you chew with your teeth, and you see with your eyes. All these parts work together to keep you alive.

▽ Inside your body, there is a framework of bones, called your skeleton. This supports your body and protects the parts inside it.

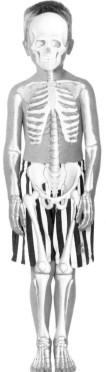

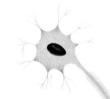

nerve cell

▷ There are millions of tiny cells in your body. They make up every part of you. This is what a muscle cell looks like when you see it through a microscope.

muscle cell

△ Nerve cells are also called neurons. They carry messages between your brain and your body. Some nerve cells are very long. The nerve cells that run down your leg to your toes can be over three feet long.

skin cell

△ Different cells have different shapes and sizes. This is what one of your skin cells looks like.

▽ Everyone's body works the same way, but no one else looks just like you!

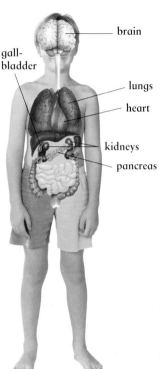

brain

gall-
bladder

lungs

heart

kidneys

pancreas

▷ Some organs link up to
form systems. Food travels
through your body along
your digestive system.
Here it is broken into tiny
bits and mixed with
chemicals. Useful parts of
the food pass into your
blood and are carried all
around your body. Your
cells need energy from
food to work.

◁ Some parts of your
body are called organs.
Each one has a job to do.
Your heart pumps blood
around your body. Your
lungs help you breathe,
and your stomach helps
you to digest your food.
Your brain lets you think
and controls the rest of
your body.

liver

stomach

intestines

▷ Like everything else inside
you, blood is made up of
cells. There are two kinds of
blood cells—red and white.
The red cells get their color
from a chemical inside them.
It carries oxygen from the air
you breathe in. All your cells
need oxygen to stay alive.
White cells help you fight
disease. Blood travels around
your body along tiny tubes
called blood vessels.

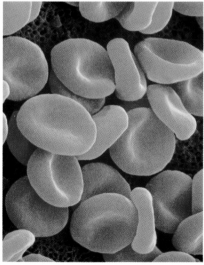

▷ Your heart pumps blood to parts of your body along arteries (colored blue). The blood goes back to your heart along veins (colored red). Then it is pumped to your lungs, and then back around your body again.

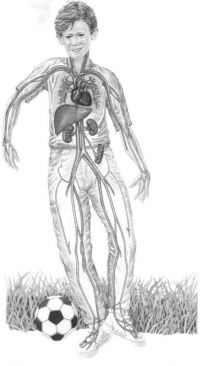

△ When you move, your muscles and bones work together. The muscles in your arm pull on the bones to make your arm bend and straighten.

◁ When you breathe, you draw air down your windpipe into your lungs. Oxygen from the air goes from your lungs into your blood and is carried to all the cells in your body. They need oxygen to stay alive.

◁ Your heart pumps blood around your body. It pumps, or beats, about once every second. Press gently on a friend's wrist. Can you feel it throb as blood surges through the blood vessel there?

Find out more

Biology
Energy
Light and Lenses
Living things
Medicine
Reproduction
Senses

Inventions and Discoveries

Every gadget we use, from paperclips to computers, had to be invented by someone. Some inventions are new ideas which no one had thought of before. Others are ideas for making older kinds of gadgets work better.

A discovery is different from an invention. It is when somebody finds out something new about the Earth or the Universe.

△ These shoes have Velcro fastenings. You close them by pressing a strip of tiny nylon hooks against a strip of tiny nylon loops. The man who invented Velcro got the idea from the way burrs (spiky seeds) stick to animals' fur.

safety pin

umbrella

early telephone

▷ Some inventions, such as the telephone, made a huge difference to people's lives. The telephone was invented by Alexander Graham Bell in 1876. Other inventions, such as the safety pin, seem less important, but they are still very useful.

△ Umbrellas were invented more than 2,000 years ago in China.

▷ Ballpoint pens were invented in 1938 by Lazlo Biro.

◁ This picture shows Sir Alexander Fleming at work in his laboratory. He discovered penicillin in 1928. This was the first antibiotic. These are drugs used to treat illnesses, such as bronchitis (a chest infection).

Find out more

Computers
Experiment
Machines
Microwaves
Recording
Technology
Television
X rays

Lasers

A laser is a machine that makes a narrow beam of light energy, called a laser beam. This is not like a beam of ordinary light. It is made from one color of light and does not spread out like ordinary light does. Lasers can be used in many ways, from cutting metal to performing delicate hospital operations.

△ In hospitals, surgeons use lasers to perform sensitive operations. Here, a laser is being used to operate on a patient's eye.

laser beam ———

△ A CD-ROM drive is a small laser inside a computer. The laser beam detects the pattern of tiny pits on the CD-ROM, which the drive turns into numbers that the computer can read.

◁ Very powerful laser beams can cut through metal sheets. The metal gets so hot when the beam hits it that it melts.

Find out more
Color
Computers
Energy
Light and Lenses
Measurement
Medicine
Recording

Light and Lenses

Without light we could not see anything. During the day, most of the light we see comes from the Sun. At night, we have artifical lights inside our homes and on the streets outside. Light usually travels in straight lines called rays. We see things because the rays hit an object, then bounce back into our eyes.

▷ Light from the Sun and lightbulbs is called white light. It is made up of different colors mixed together. Things look colored because they only reflect (bounce back) some of these colors and not others.

◁ Light travels in straight lines called rays. If the rays cannot reach a surface because there is something stopping them, a shadow forms. Your hand makes a shadow on the wall because it stops the light from reaching the wall.

▷ Light rays can be bent or made to change direction. When you put a straw into a glass, it looks bent. This is because the rays of light reflected from the straw bend when they leave the water and pass into the air.

▽ This desert traveler can see a welcome pool of water in front of the palm trees. But the water is not really there. This is called a mirage. It happens when layers of warm air near the ground bend rays of light from the bright sky.

△ Like sunlight, the light from this flashlight is a mix of many colors. When the girl shines the flashlight on the green balloon, the balloon soaks up all the colors in the light, except green. Green light bounces back into the girl's eyes and she sees a green balloon.

◁ Some creatures, such as this glow worm, can produce light from their own bodies. The light is not to help the glow worm see. It is to attract a mate.

◁ A magnifying glass makes things look bigger. It does this by bending the straight rays of light as they pass through the glass lens.

▽ A telescope makes objects in the distance look larger. If you point a telescope at the night sky, you can see many more stars than you can with your eyes alone. This is because the telescope collects a lot more light than your eyes can collect.

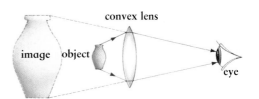

convex lens

image   object   eye

△ A magnifying glass works like this. When rays of light pass through the lens, they are bent inward, toward each other. When they reach your eye they seem to be coming from a much larger object.

convex lens

concave lens

△ A lens that bulges in the middle is called a convex lens. When rays of light pass through it, they bend inward, toward each other. A magnifying glass has a convex lens.

▽ A lens that is thinner in the middle is called a concave lens. Rays of light passing through it spread outward. If you look at something through a concave lens, it often looks smaller than it really is.

▷ A microscope makes things look much bigger than a magnifying glass does. It has lots of lenses inside, and can make things look hundreds of times bigger than they really are. This scientist is using a microscope to examine some of the tiny living things that cause disease.

◁ With some people, the rays of light passing into their eyes do not bend enough to make a clear picture. With others, the rays may bend too much. The lenses in eyeglasses help people to see more clearly by correcting the amount the rays are bent.

Find out more
Color
Day and Night
Energy
Lasers
Mirrors
Senses
Television

Liquids

Water, orange juice, oil, and molasses are all types of liquids. Liquids are one of the three states of matter. The others are solids and gases. Liquid are like gases in some ways. They can flow from one place to another, and change shape to fit the container they are in. But they cannot be squashed, as gases can. The most common liquid on Earth is water.

△ The surface of a liquid acts like a slightly stretchy elastic skin. Very light things, such as this water strider, can rest on the skin without falling through.

liquid

gas

solid

△ The molecules (particles) that make up a gas move around all the time. The molecules in solids cling together and cannot move. The molecules in liquids cling a little, but they can still move around.

▽ Pour some water into different shaped containers. What happens? The water changes shape, to fill the bottom of the container.

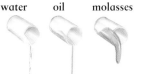

water   oil   molasses

△ Some liquids are runnier than others. Water is thin and flows easily. Molasses is thick and flows slowly. Is the oil in the picture thicker than molasses, or thinner?

Find out more
Chemistry and Chemicals
Floating
Friction
Gases
Solids
Water

◁ This liquid is very hot iron. Iron is normally a solid metal but when it gets very hot it melts and becomes liquid. When it cools, it turns into a solid again.

Living things

A living thing grows, feeds, breathes, and can reproduce (make young). The two main types of living things are plants and animals. Animals are living things that can move around. They eat other living things as food. Plants are living things that stay in one place. They make their own food using the energy from sunlight.

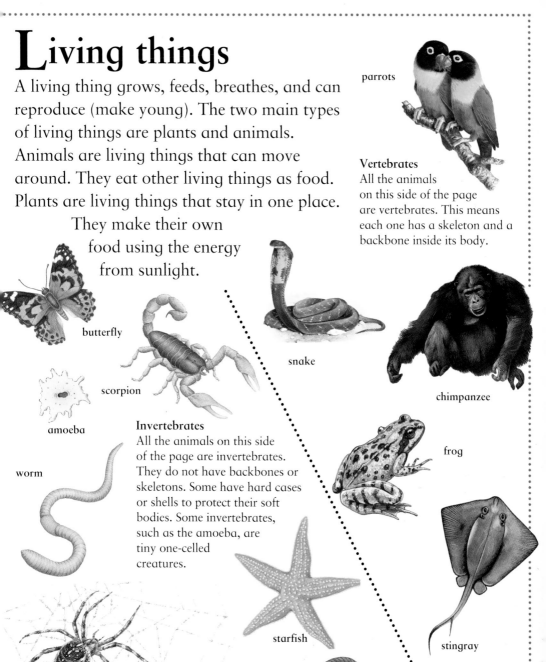

parrots

Vertebrates
All the animals on this side of the page are vertebrates. This means each one has a skeleton and a backbone inside its body.

butterfly

scorpion

snake

chimpanzee

amoeba

Invertebrates
All the animals on this side of the page are invertebrates. They do not have backbones or skeletons. Some have hard cases or shells to protect their soft bodies. Some invertebrates, such as the amoeba, are tiny one-celled creatures.

worm

frog

stingray

starfish

spider

snail

▽ Plants use energy from sunlight, and water and minerals from the soil to make their own food. Many plants make flowers seeds. The seeds grow into new plants.

flower
stem
leaf
root

△ Some animals, such as this bear, hibernate in the winter. This means that they go into a kind of deep sleep. This saves energy, as they do not need to hunt for food.

▽ Sea anemones look like plants but are really animals. They use their tentacles to catch small creatures to eat.

▽ There are hundreds of thousands of different kinds of plants. Some are so tiny that you can only see them through a microscope. Others, such as trees, can be huge.

△ Animals must find food to eat, or they will die. Some animals eat plants. Others, like this fish eagle, eat animals. Some animals, such as humans, eat both plants and animals.

Habitats

Arctic

desert

Fact box

• Scientists know of about 400,000 different species of plants. But they also know there are many more, waiting to be discovered.

• The blue whale is the biggest animal that has ever lived. It is bigger than any of the dinosaurs.

rain forest

grassy plain

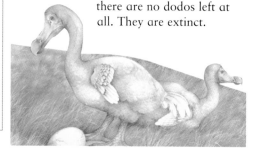

▽ Dodos were a kind of bird that lived on a small island in the Indian Ocean. People killed so many for food that now there are no dodos left at all. They are extinct.

◁ Rhinoceroses are in danger of becoming extinct (dying out). One reason for this is because so many have been killed by hunters for their precious horns. This rhinoceros's horns have been cut off, to protect it.

◁ The places where plants and animals live are called their habitats. Animals and plants are usually specially suited to their particular habitats. Arctic animals have thick coats to keep them warm in the icy cold. Desert plants and animals need very little water to stay alive.

Find out more

Air and
Atmosphere
Day and Night
Earth
Human body
Medicine
Senses
Water

◁ Rain forests are home to about half of all the types of plants and animals in the world. In the grassy plains of Africa, hunters, such as lions, lie in wait to prey on antelopes and zebras.

Machines

Machines are things that make jobs easier and quicker to do. Some machines are very simple. For example, a hammer is a simple machine—so is a wheelbarrow, and so is a pair of scissors. People have used simple machines like these for thousands of years.

▽ 1 Make and use a simple machine. Start by putting some heavy books on a table. Try lifting them with your finger. It's hard work. Next, slide one end of a ruler under the books.

1

△ A slope does not look much like a machine. But it can be used as one because it makes getting to a high point easier than climbing straight upward.

▷ 2 Lift up the end of the ruler. This makes the books much easier to move. The ruler is working as a machine called a lever. We often use levers to help us lift things.

2

pliers

▽ Many of the machines we use at home need electricity to make them work.

wheelbarrow

can opener

◁ Pliers, a wheelbarrow, and a can opener are all examples of levers. When you push or pull one part of a lever, such as the pliers' handles, you make a push or pull on another part, such as the pliers' tips.

hairdryer

vacuum cleaner

◁ A pulley is a machine that helps you to lift heavy objects. It is made of a rope that runs around one or more wheels. As you pull down on one end of the rope, the other end rises and lifts whatever is attached to it.

△ A combine harvester is a complicated machine made of several machines rolled into one. It cuts the corn and threshes it, to get the grain from the straw (stems). Then it packs the straw into bales.

▷ Cars, aircraft, and trains are all transportation machines that move people and goods from place to place. They all have engines that turn fuel into energy, to turn their wheels or make them fly.

◁ A bicycle is made up of many simple machines that work together. For example, the pedals and gears are simple machines that make pedaling easier. The brakes are simple machines to help slow the wheels down.

Find out more
Energy
Engines
Force
Technology

Magnets

Have you ever tried to pick up a piece of paper with a magnet? It can't be done! Magnets can only pick up things made from certain kinds of metals. The most common of these are iron and steel. The force or pull that magnets exert is called magnetic force.

△ The area around a magnet is called its magnetic field. This is as far as its power stretches. To see a magnetic field, put a magnet on a sheet of paper and sprinkle some iron filings around it. The filings cluster inside the magnetic field, around the magnet's poles (ends).

 fridge magnet

▽ One end of the magnet is called its north pole and the other is its south pole. Two north poles facing each other push each other apart. So do two south poles facing each other. But if a north pole faces a south pole, they pull towards each other.

fridge magnet

◁ The needle in a compass is actually a magnet. It swings around until its north pole points north—toward the Earth's magnetic north pole.

△ The Earth has its own magnetic field. It is as if the Earth has a huge bar-shaped magnet running through it, with its poles near the Earth's North and South poles.

the Earth's magnetic field

◁ Make some fish from tinfoil. Fix a paperclip to each one. Make two toy fishing rods by tying magnets to pieces of string. Have a competition with a friend. Dangle the rods above the fish. Who catches the most?

▽ This train travels by floating along, just above a rail. There is a magnet inside the train and the rail is a magnet, too. The two magnets are arranged so that they push each other away. Because of this, the train floats above the rail as it moves.

1

◁ **1** You can make a magnet using electricity. This kind of magnet is called an electromagnet. You need some thin plastic-covered wire, a steel nail, and a flashlight battery. Start by winding the wire around the nail. Wind all the way up and down the nail until the wire is about three layers thick.

fridge magnet

2

▷ **2** Fix one end of the wire to the top of the battery and the other end to the bottom, so that you have made a circuit. Now try picking up a paperclip or a steel thumbtack with the nail. What happens when you disconnect the battery?

Find out more
Battery
Earth
Electricity
Force
Machines
Materials
Recording
Television

Materials

Look around your classroom. Can you see clothes, shoes, chairs, tables, and books? What are these things made of? Some are made of plastic, and others are made of metal, wood, or fabrics. These are all materials. Different materials have different uses. For example, shoes are often made from leather or plastic because these are strong but will bend.

▷ These things are made from clay. Clay is a kind of soft earth that can be formed into different shapes. When it is baked it becomes very hard. Things made from clay are called ceramics.

Make a kite

tape

garden canes

plastic sheet

ribbons

◁ What sort of materials would you use to make a kite like this one? Remember, a kite must be made of something light, so it will fly. It must be strong, so that it does not tear in the wind.

△ This kite's frame is made from thin garden canes. It is covered with sheets of plastic. The flying line is light, strong fishing line.

◁ Everything in this picture is made from plastic. Plastics are synthetic materials, which means they are made in factories, from chemicals.

Some kinds of plastics are hard and stiff. Others are soft and bend.

△ Reusing materials instead of throwing them away is called recycling. For example, these bottles are going to be recycled. They may be used again, or the glass may be melted down to make new bottles.

▷ Fabric is a word for cloth. Fabrics are made by weaving or knitting fibers (thin strands) together. Wool and cotton are called natural fibers because they come from animals or plants. Synthetic fibers, such as nylon, are made from chemicals.

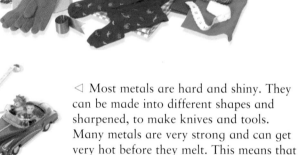

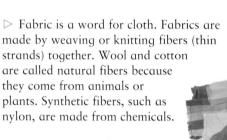

◁ Most metals are hard and shiny. They can be made into different shapes and sharpened, to make knives and tools. Many metals are very strong and can get very hot before they melt. This means that they are a good material for saucepans.

◁ In many parts of the world, the materials people use in their everyday lives are the ones they can find nearby. For example, these boats are made from reeds that grow on the lake where their owners live.

Find out more
Environment
Fuels
Technology

Mathematics

Mathematics is the study of numbers and how we use them. Most people use some mathematics every day, to count their money, add up their shopping bill, measure things, or keep the score in sports. Many people use mathematics in their work. For example, scientists and engineers use mathematics to make calculations and keep records of their results.

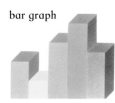

▷ Mathematicians sometimes use charts and graphs to show information in ways that are easier to understand than long lists of numbers.

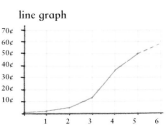

line graph

△ Do you do problems like these at school? Adding, subtracting, multiplying, and dividing is called arithmetic. Arithmetic is just one part of mathematics.

Fact box
• The Ancient Egyptians used geometry to help them design the pyramids.

△ This line graph shows how someone's allowance went up over six years.

pie chart   bar graph

△ Pie charts and bar graphs can be used to show what someone bought with their allowance. Each color stands for a different item, such as candy or toys.

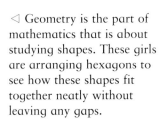

◁ Geometry is the part of mathematics that is about studying shapes. These girls are arranging hexagons to see how these shapes fit together neatly without leaving any gaps.

Find out more
Calculator
Experiment
Numbers

Measurement

How can you tell how long, how tall, how heavy, how hot, or how cold something is? The answer is by measuring it.

Measurements are made in units. For example, we use pounds and ounces for weight, feet and inches for length, and degrees for temperature.

△ In some countries, people measure long distances in kilometers. In others, they use miles. These road signs in Australia and the United States show both. Eight kilometers is equal to five miles.

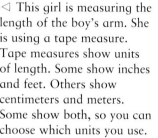

◁ This girl is measuring the length of the boy's arm. She is using a tape measure. Tape measures show units of length. Some show inches and feet. Others show centimeters and meters. Some show both, so you can choose which units you use.

△ The amount of space something takes up is called its volume. This cup is for measuring the volume of liquids. The units used are pints or liters.

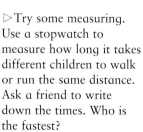

▷ Try some measuring. Use a stopwatch to measure how long it takes different children to walk or run the same distance. Ask a friend to write down the times. Who is the fastest?

Find out more
Clocks
Hot and Cold
Mathematics
Numbers

Medicine

Medicine is the study of health, disease, and injury. When someone is sick, they might ask a doctor for help. The doctor uses a knowledge of medicine to find out what is wrong, and help the patient to get better. Many illnesses can be cured with chemicals, called drugs. These are also sometimes called medicines.

▽ Sometimes, a sick person needs an operation. A doctor called a surgeon makes a cut to reach inside the body. A drug called an anesthetic is used to stop the person feeling any pain.

◁ This picture shows the first time doctors used antiseptics. These are chemicals that kill germs. Antiseptics were first used in operations in 1867. Before this, people often died after operations from infections caused by germs.

acanthus

chicory

△ For thousands of years, people have used special plants to treat sickness. Many modern drugs also contain chemicals found in plants.

△ Sometimes doctors give us injections containing a special kind of drug, called a vaccine. Vaccines help to stop us from catching diseases, such as measles.

Never touch or swallow any medicines or plants unless they are given to you by an adult.

Find out more
Biology
Chemistry and Chemicals
Technology
X rays

Melting and Boiling

Melting is when a solid turns into a liquid. Boiling turns liquid into a gas. These are called changes of state because they change a substance from one state of matter to another. A substance needs heat to make it melt or boil. There are two other changes of state. When gases cool, they may condense and become liquid. Liquids can be turned into solids by cooling or freezing.

△ What happens if you don't eat your Popsicle quickly enough? It melts in the warm air. The solid ice turns to liquid.

Warning! Never touch or move anything with hot or boiling liquid in it. You could get badly burned.

△ This beaker is full of nitrogen. Nitrogen is normally a gas, but if it is made very cold it condenses and turns into a liquid. In this picture, you can see it turning back into a gas in the warm air.

△ When you heat water, it gets hotter and hotter until the temperature reaches 212°F (100°C). It then boils and starts to turn into a gas called water vapor.

◁ Watch how a gas turns into liquid when it is cooled. Breathe onto a mirror. Water vapor in your breath cools when it reaches the surface of the mirror and turns into liquid (water).

Find out more
Energy
Gases
Hot and Cold
Liquids
Solids

Microwaves

Do you have a microwave oven in your kitchen? Microwaves are used in cooking, but they can also carry messages and signals through air and space. Satellite television programs are carried by microwaves. When you make an international telephone call, microwaves may carry the call up to a communications satellite in space, and then back down to Earth.

△ The dishes at the top of this tower send and pick up microwaves. These carry long-distance telephone calls.

Never put anything in a microwave oven without asking an adult first.

▽ This is a microwave oven. Microwaves are beamed into the food. They make the atoms in the food move around. When this happens, the food gets hot and cooks.

▷ There is a machine inside the oven that makes the microwaves.

fan

microwaves

◁ A fan scatters the microwaves around so that they reach every part of the food being cooked.

▷ Ships and aircraft use radar to detect objects around them. A radar dish sends out beams of microwaves. If these strike an object, they bounce back to the dish and the object shows up on a screen linked to the dish.

Find out more
Hot and Cold
Light and Lenses
Radio
X rays

Mirrors

A mirror is a smooth, shiny surface that reflects nearly all the light that hits it. You can see yourself in a mirror because light reflects from you to the mirror and then bounces off the mirror and back into your eyes. Most mirrors are made of glass. Mirrors are not simply for looking at yourself. They have many other uses, too.

△ The back of a mirror is painted silver. Light bounces off this smooth layer of silver paint and into your eyes.

◁ How many other shiny surfaces can you find? Metals are very shiny. Other very smooth things, such as china plates, are shiny, too.

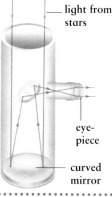

▷ Astronomers use large, powerful telescopes to look at the stars. These have mirrors inside them. The mirrors are curved like shallow dishes. They work in the same sort of way as lenses, to make things look nearer.

light from stars

eye-piece

curved mirror

△ Look at your reflection in a mirror. The mirror reflects your image straight out again so everything looks backwards. See if you can work out how this happens.

Find out more
Lasers
Light and Lenses

Motion

Motion is another word for movement. Things cannot start to move on their own. They need a force (a push or a pull) to get them started. Once something has started to move, a force can make it move faster, or it can slow it down again. Speeding up motion is called acceleration. Slowing it down is called deceleration.

△ This shot-putter uses force to get the shot moving through the air. Gravity pulls at the shot as it travels along. It slows the shot down and then pulls it back to the ground.

◁ **1** A moving object will always try to keep moving, and a still object will try to stay still. This is called inertia. Try this experiment. Put a raw egg on a tray and spin it. As the egg spins, the runny yolk inside it spins, too.

▷ **2** Stop the egg, then quickly let go of it. It starts to spin again. This is because the yoke inside the egg has inertia. It goes on moving when you stop the shell. When you let go of the shell, inertia starts the egg moving again.

△ The faster a car is going, the longer it takes for it to stop. That is why it is important for drivers to go slowly in places where people may be crossing the street.

▷ Moving objects always try to keep going in a straight line. The boy is swinging the weight on the end of this string in a circle. The weight needs a force to keep it moving in a circle. The force comes from the string. Without it, the weight would fly off in a straight line.

△ These heavy railroad cars need a lot of force to make them move. The locomotives had to exert a huge pull on them to get them started. Heavy things are harder to get moving and harder to slow down than light things.

▽ A grasshopper is light and small. Its legs give a huge push compared to its size, which helps it to accelerate very fast when it hops away.

Find out more
Energy
Flight
Force

Nuclear energy

Everything that exists is made up of atoms. An atom is made up of a nucleus, surrounded by electrons. If a nucleus breaks apart, a huge amount of energy is released. This is called nuclear energy. In a nuclear power plant this is used to make electricity. When atoms break apart, they also give out rays called radioactivity. Things that give off radioactivity are called radioactive.

△ Massive amounts of energy are formed in the Sun. There, atoms join together instead of splitting apart. This is another way that nuclear energy is created.

◁ Inside a nuclear power plant, nuclear reactors split atoms apart and release energy as heat. This heat is used to produce electrical energy.

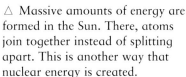

▷ This sign means "Danger! Radioactivity!" It is used wherever there are radioactive substances. These can be very dangerous, causing burns and diseases in people and animals.

▷ An atom bomb makes a massive explosion. Billions of atoms split up at the same time and an enormous amount of energy is released. After the explosion, dangerous nuclear radiation is left behind for many years.

Find out more
Atoms
Energy
Fuels
Solar System
Universe

Numbers

We use numbers in many different ways. We use them for counting, for writing down measurements, and for doing problems. We also use them for labeling things, such as the houses in a street and telephone numbers.

Numbers are shown as symbols, called digits. For example, the number 368 has three digits—3, 6, and 8.

△ The numbers we use today were invented in India over 1,000 years ago. Arab traders started using them and brought them to Europe.

▽ We count and do problems using numbers in groups. For example, in 235, the 2 means two hundreds, the 3 means three tens, and the 5 means five ones. This system of numbers is called base ten.

2 hundreds

3 tens

5 ones

△ Around the world people write numbers differently. They were also different in the past. Medieval numbers were used in Europe in the 1100s and 1200s. Roman numbers are still used today.

Fact box
• Before numbers were invented, people carved a notch on a stick or bone to keep count of things. Sometimes, they made a pile of stones instead. Count ng this way is called keeping a tally.

▷ Computers do calculations using a system of numbers called the binary system. They use only two digits— 0 and 1. Here you can see how to write the numbers 0 to 8 in the binary system.

binary numbers

Find out more
Calculator
Clocks
Computers
Mathematics
Measurement

Physics

Physics is the study of how the universe works, and how and why things happen in it. People who study physics are called physicists. They study things such as why objects move when they are pushed, how electricity works, and why things melt when they are heated. Some physicists try to find out what happens inside atoms and what the universe is made of.

△ Physicists make important discoveries. About 300 years ago, Italian scientist Galileo dropped objects from the Tower of Pisa to show that heavy things do not fall faster than light ones.

Mechanics This is the study of how things move.

Electricity Physicists study how electricity works.

Optics Studying optics means finding out about light.

Energy Physicists study how energy makes things happen.

Sound Physicists study how sound travels from place to place.

heat (and cold)

Heat Studying heat means finding out about melting, boiling, and how things get hot or cold.

Find out more
Light and Lenses
Melting and Boiling
Motion

Pressure

When you press something, you put pressure on it. Pressure is measured by how much force is being put on a certain area of a surface. If a force is spread over a large area, there is less pressure than if the same force is all put on a small area. Liquids and gases also exert pressure. For example, there is pressure on the seabed because of the huge weight of water pressing down from above.

△ This pump squeezes air into a balloon. This makes more pressure on the inside of the balloon than on the outside, so the balloon stretches.

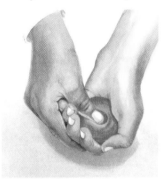

◁ **1** Squash some modeling clay with your thumb. You have to press hard to make a dent in the clay.

▽ Pressure in the water pipes pushes water out of a tap or a shower. If you put your finger over the holes, you can feel the pressure building up.

△ This vehicle has wide tires that spread the vehicle's weight over a large area of the ground. This keeps the pressure low and stops the vehicle from sinking.

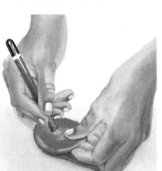

△ **2** Try pushing a pencil into the clay. It goes in much more easily because the pressure is high at the sharp point.

Find out more
Air and Atmosphere
Force
Gases
Solids

Radio

Radio is a way of sending messages over long distances. Sounds are turned into waves, called radio waves. These travel from one place to another through air and space. You cannot see them because they are invisible. Radio waves are also used to send signals from radio and television stations, and to carry messages to and from cellular telephones.

△ The aerial on a radio picks up radio waves coming from a transmitter. The radio turns the waves back into sound.

◁ In a radio station, music and other sounds are turned into an electrical signal. This signal goes to a transmitter, which turns it into radio waves.

▷ A walkie-talkie turns the sound of your voice into radio waves. The waves travel to another walkie-talkie which turns them back into sound.

△ This is a radio telescope. It picks up radio waves coming from space. Astronomers study these waves to find out things about the Universe that they cannot learn from ordinary telescopes.

Find out more
Electricity
Microwaves
Sound
Telephones

Recording

Recording something means storing it in a way that makes it possible to see or hear it again and again. We can record voices, music, and pictures.

When we talk about recording, we usually mean recording sound. What we actually record are vibrations in the air. We can do this with a tape recorder.

△ 1 When you record your voice, a microphone turns sound (vibrations in the air) into an electrical signal. The signal is recorded on the tape in the tape recorder.

this head wipes the magnetic pattern off the tape before a new recording is made

record and playback head

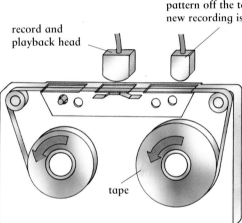

tape

◁ 2 The tape in a tape recorder has a special magnetic coating. When a recording is being made, an electromagnet in the recorder makes an invisible pattern on the tape.

Fact box

• Many airplanes have flight recorders that record the airplane's movements during a flight. A cockpit voice recorder records what the pilots say during the flight as well.

△3 To play a recording, the tape recorder turns the invisible patterns into an electrical signal. This signal goes to a loudspeaker, which turns it into sound.

▷ On a compact disc (CD), sounds are recorded as a pattern of tiny pits in the surface. A laser beam in the player reads this pattern and the electronics inside the player turn it into sound.

Find out more
Electricity
Lasers
Magnets
Sound
Video

Reproduction

Plants make seeds that grow into new plants. Animals have babies that grow into adults. This is called reproduction. It means making new plants and animals that live on when their parents die. Usually, two plants or animals, one female and one male, are needed for reproduction.

△ For a plant to make seeds, a male flower's pollen has to join with a female flower's ovary. Some plants have both male and female flowers. Others need insects to carry pollen from flower to flower. These flowers are bee-shaped to attract bees to their pollen.

Fact box
• Some fish lay millions of eggs. This way they make sure that some, at least, survive and grow.
• Blue whales have the biggest young of all animals. A newborn baby weighs 5 tons.

▷ This foal is drinking milk from its mother. The milk contains everything the foal needs to grow strong and healthy. Horses are mammals. All mammal mothers produce milk for their young at the start of their lives.

amoeba

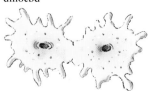

△ Some living things are very small and simple. They are made up of just one cell. Instead of having young, they reproduce by splitting in two.

baby in uterus

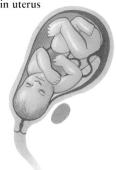

◁ Before you were born, you spent nine months growing inside your mother's uterus. You grew from two tiny cells, an egg from your mother and a sperm cell from your father.

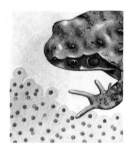   

△ Amphibians reproduce in water. A female frog, for example, lays hundreds of eggs in the water. Then the male fertilizes (adds his sperm to) them.

△ Tadpoles form inside the eggs and then hatch out. They do not look like frogs, yet. They look more like fish.

△ Gradually, the tadpoles grow legs and lose their tails.

△ This young frog is now ready to leave the water.

◁ **1** Female birds lay eggs. The egg has a hard shell to protect the baby growing inside. It also has a store of food in its yolk.

embryo (bird beginning to form)

▽ This is a seed beginning to grow into a new plant. It grows roots first, then a shoot, and then leaves.

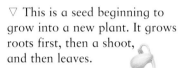

▷ **2** The parent birds sit on the egg to keep it warm as the baby bird grows inside.

young bird growing

▷ **3** At last, the baby bird is ready to hatch. It pecks at the shell to break it, and then squeezes out.

young bird

Find out more

Flight
Human body
Living things
Water

Satellites

A satellite is an object in space that travels around another object, such as a planet. This is called being in orbit. The Moon is a natural satellite that has orbited the Earth for billions of years. The other satellites orbiting the Earth are made by people. They are launched into orbit by space rockets. Some watch and measure the weather, some are used for communications, and some investigate outer space.

Communications satellites can carry telephone messages through space to the other side of the world. A message is beamed up from Earth to the satellite and then back down again to a receiver, which can be thousands of miles away from the caller.

▽ This satellite looks for cosmic rays. Its solar panels turn sunlight into electricity that the satellite needs to work. Its aerial sends information back to Earth. It also has thrusters, like tiny rockets, that turn the satellite to point in different directions.

radiation detector

aerial

solar panels

signals

◁ The Hubble space telescope is a satellite that takes pictures of objects far out in space and sends them back to Earth. This picture shows the space shuttle (and reuseable space rocket) putting the telescope into orbit high above the Earth.

Find out more
Energy
Radio
Solar System
Space travel
Telephones
Universe
Weather

Seasons

Different parts of the Earth have different seasons throughout the year. This means that the weather changes according to the time of year. Some places have a warm season called summer, a cold one called winter, and in between these, they have autumn and spring. In other places it may be warm all year long, with a rainy season and a dry season.

▷ As summer ends, autumn begins. The weather gets cooler and the days get shorter. Deciduous trees lose their leaves. Some birds migrate to warmer countries. Other animals, such as bears, go into a deep sleep called hibernation until the spring comes.

△ In the spring, the weather warms up after the cold winter months. The days begin to get longer and lighter. Seeds begin to sprout, and trees grow new leaves. Spring flowers bloom and many baby animals are born.

Earth tilting on its axis

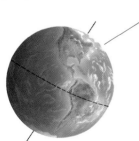

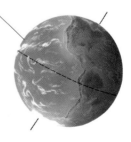

△ The Earth tilts, like this. When the northern half tilts toward the Sun, it has summer. The days are long and the nights are short. In the south, meanwhile, it is winter. The days are short and the nights are long.

△ Here, the southern half of the Earth tilts toward the Sun. It has summer now. The days are long and the nights are short. In the north, meanwhile, it is winter, with short days and long nights.

Find out more
Day and Night
Earth
Solar System
Weather

Senses

How do you know what is happening around you, or what something feels like, or smells like? The answer is that you use your senses. Humans have five senses. These are sight, hearing, touch, taste, and smell. We often use more than one sense at a time. For example, when you eat something, you smell and taste it at the same time—and see it, too.

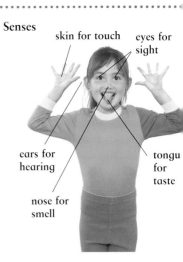

Senses

skin for touch

eyes for sight

ears for hearing

tongue for taste

nose for smell

▷ **1** Get a friend to guess what something is just by using his or her sense of touch. Cut a hole in the side of a large cardboard box. Make it big enough to put an arm through. Find a few different objects to put in the box.

△ Your sense organs pick up tastes, touches, smells, sounds, and sights. They send messages about these along your nerves to your brain. Your brain sorts out these messages and tells you what is going on around you.

Fact box

• Not everyone's senses work in the same way. For example, there are people who cannot easily tell red and green colors apart. This is because the light-sensitive cells in their eyes do not work properly.

△ **2** Do not let your friend see what the objects are. Can your friend tell what each one is just by feeling it through the hole?

△ Can you see the line of dots along the side of this fish? They act like another pair of eyes and detect movements made by other creatures nearby in the water. This helps the fish to find food and to escape from enemies.

▷ Many bats use their superb sense of hearing to find food and other objects in the dark. The bat makes clicking sounds as it flies. These sounds bounce off objects, making echoes that the bat uses to tell where and what the objects are.

▽ One boy bursts a balloon, and the other boy points to where the sound is coming from. He hears the sound more loudly in one ear than the other. This tells him where the sound is being made.

△ Dogs have a much better sense of smell than humans. This dog has been trained to use its sense of smell to search for explosives.

△ This person's sense of sight does not work properly, so her guide dog helps her to find her way around.

Find out more
Color
Human body
Light and Lenses
Sound

Solar System

The Solar System is made up of the Sun and the nine planets that orbit (travel around) it. One of these planets is the Earth. Some of these planets have moons orbiting around them. Comets and asteroids travel around the Solar System, too. As far as we know, the Earth is the only place in the Solar System where anything lives.

△ The Earth has one moon. It is nearly 240,000 miles from Earth. Its diameter is only a quarter of the Earth's.

Never look straight at the Sun, either with binoculars or just with your eyes.

◁ Try looking at the Moon through a pair of binoculars. Can you see the craters on the surface?

The Solar System is enormous. If the Sun was only the size of a football, the Earth would be the size of a pinhead, 80 feet away. Pluto would be about a mile from the Sun.

▷ Jupiter and Saturn are huge. They are made of gas and liquid. Jupiter is the biggest of all the planets. The others could all fit inside it easily.

Jupiter

▽ Mercury, Venus, Earth, and Mars are small, rocky planets. Mercury is nearest to the Sun.

Mercury

Venus

Earth

Mars

▽ This is the spacecraft Voyager 2. It is a space probe. It was sent from Earth in 1977 to explore outer space. It reached Neptune in 1989. Scientists have learned a lot about planets from Voyager 2 and other spacecraft like it.

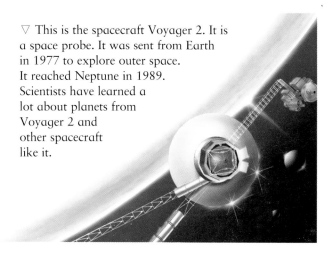

▷ If you are lucky, you might see streaks of light, called shooting stars or meteors, in the night sky. They are made by rocks called meteors hurtling into the Earth's atmosphere and burning up.

Saturn

◁ Some planets have rings of solid material around them. Jupiter and Neptune have rings of dust. Uranus has rings of rocks. Saturn has the most rings. They are made up of millions of lumps of ice.

▽ Pluto is the farthest planet from the Sun. It is smaller than the Earth's moon.

Uranus

Neptune

• **Pluto**

Find out more
Earth
Satellites
Space travel
Universe

Solids

A solid is one of the three states of matter. The others are liquids and gases. A solid has a fixed shape. It does not flow around like a liquid or a gas. This is because the atoms are joined firmly together, and can hardly move around at all.

△ In some solids, the atoms are arranged in neat rows. This sort of solid is called a crystal.

◁ **1** This is how to make sugar crystals grow. Stir some sugar into warm water until no more will dissolve.

▷ **2** Pour the liquid into a saucer and leave it in a warm place, so that the water evaporates. Can you see the crystals beginning to form?

△ These objects are made from solids that are not crystals. Although their atoms are not in neat rows, they still cannot move around.

▽ Some solids are softer than others. The soft, gray substance in pencils is called graphite. It rubs easily onto the paper when you write.

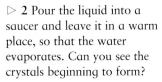

△ Diamond and graphite are both made of carbon, but their atoms are arranged in a different way. Diamond is extremely hard. It is used in jewelry and to make tools for cutting, such as drills.

Find out more
Atoms
Gases
Liquids
Materials

Sound

Sound is made by vibrations. When you speak, you make vibrations in the air. These vibrations spread out. Anyone whose ears can pick up the vibrations will hear the sound of your voice. Sound can travel through solids and liquids as well as through air and other gases.

▽ To see the vibrations that give us sound, cover a plastic pot with a piece of balloon, and secure it with a rubber band. Sprinkle salt on it. Speak near the balloon. The vibrations will make the salt grains jump up and down.

Loudness

rocket on takeoff 150–190 decibels

◁ The loudness of a sound depends on the size of the vibrations it makes. Sounds are loud when the vibrations are very big, and soft when they are small. Loudness is measured in units called decibels. The noise of a road drill is over 100 decibels.

motorcycle 70–90 decibels

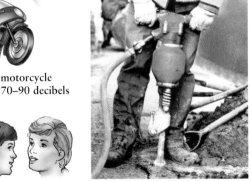

talking quietly 30–60 decibels

▽ As sound spreads, the molecules making up the air are squashed together, pulled apart, squashed again, and so on, making sound waves.

△ This road drill makes a very loud noise. Sounds this loud can damage people's ears. The workers using the drill must cover their ears to protect them.

leaves rustling 20 decibels

A sound can be high-pitched or low-pitched. The pitch of a sound (how high it is) depends on its frequency (the number of vibrations it makes per second).

▷ Try this experiment to make high- and low-pitched sounds. Pour some water into jars, so that the level is different in each. Tap the jars with a pen. Which jar makes the sound with the highest pitch?

▷ Sonar is a way of finding things under water, using sound. A sonar machine on a ship sends "blip" sounds into the water. When these hit an object, they bounce back as echoes. The farther away the object is, the longer the echo takes to return to the control ship.

"blip"

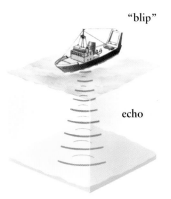

echo

Fact box

• A rocket taking off makes a sound a million times louder than a clap of thunder.
• Some animals can hear sounds that are too high- or low-pitched for human beings to hear.

◁ Some dolphins make clicking sounds and then listen for their echoes. This helps them to find their way around in murky water. It works in a similar way to sonar. Some kinds of whales communicate with each other using sound. The noises they make can travel hundreds of miles across the oceans.

▷ This brass horn looks like a long, coiled tube with a funnel. It makes a sound when the musician blows into the tube and the air inside it vibrates. The funnel spreads the sound out so you can hear it. Do you know any other brass instruments?

△ The cello is a stringed instrument. It makes a sound when the strings vibrate from side to side. This happens when a musician draws a bow across the strings or plucks them. Guitars and violins are also stringed instruments.

△ This girl is playing a flute. The boy is playing a whistle. Both of these are wind instruments. Like brass instruments, these make a sound when the musician blows into them and the air in the tube vibrates.

◁ This girl is playing an electronic keyboard. Keyboards like these are sometimes called synthesizers. A synthesizer makes sounds through a loudspeaker. Each key makes a note of a different pitch.

Find out more
Energy
Physics
Senses

Space travel

Astronauts travel into space in spacecraft. They go there for many reasons, such as to repair satellites and do experiments. Outside the spacecraft they carry a supply of air and wear spacesuits to protect them from the cold and the Sun's rays.

Astronauts have been to the Moon, but not yet to any of the planets.

◁ **1** Find out how a rocket works. Thread string through a straw, then stretch the string tightly across a room. Blow up a balloon. Hold the neck of the balloon so no air escapes, but do not tie a knot in the end of it.

△ This is a space shuttle blasting off into space. Powerful rockets send out a stream of gas and carry the shuttle into the air. To get into orbit, a spacecraft needs to travel at 17,500 miles per hour.

▷ **2** Use tape to attach the balloon to the straw. Make sure the tape touches the straw and the balloon only, and not the string.

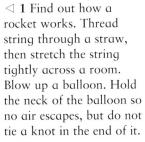

◁ **3** Make sure the balloon is still full of air. Then pull it and the straw to one end of the string. Let it go. The escaping air from the balloon pushes the straw along the string, just as a rocket pushes a spacecraft.

▷ The space shuttle carries astronauts into space, and launches satellites and space probes. It orbits the Earth and returns there after one or two weeks. It can be sent back into space again, later.

▽ In space, people float around because they are weightless. On Earth, they practice being like this in a swimming pool. Floating in water feels a little like floating in space.

◁ A space station is a spacecraft that stays in orbit around the Earth. Scientists live there for months and carry out experiments.

▽ Living on a space station can cause problems. Even eating can be tricky because food and drink float away if you are not careful.

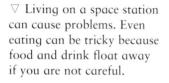

◁ It took astronauts two days to get to the Moon. A lunar module carried them from their spacecraft to the Moon's surface and back. You can see it in this picture. Some astronauts traveled around the Moon's surface in a buggy called a Lunar Rover.

Technology

Technology means designing and using tools and machines. It also means the tools and machines themselves. Computers, cars, can openers, and cameras are all examples of technology. We use technology at home, at school and when we travel from place to place. At work, technology helps people do their jobs more quickly and easily. Some technology is very complicated. Some is very simple.

△ Computer technology can help people with disabilities. For example, people who cannot use their hands can talk into a computer and it will write what they say.

△ Above are some of the different kinds of technology that people have in their homes. There is a television, a radio, a telephone, a computer, and a VCR. What kinds of technology do you have in your home?

▷ Building technology is used to design houses, tunnels, dams, and bridges. Choosing the right materials and making the design strong and safe are important parts of building technology. This is the Bay Bridge in San Francisco.

◁ Modern technology began toward the end of the 1700s. This early steam engine, the *Adler*, opened the first German public railway in 1835. The first engines reached speeds of 30 to 40 miles per hour, which people thought was amazingly fast.

▷ These people lived thousands of years ago. They built homes from clay, wood, and straw, using simple technology that suited these materials. People in many parts of the world still build in this way.

◁ This machine is called a shaduf. It is used in Egypt and other parts of the Middle East to take water from rivers to nearby fields. People have been using shadufs for over 3,000 years. The design has not changed because it works well and is easy to look after.

Find out more
Calculator
Computers
Engines
Inventions and
Discoveries
Machines

Telephones

If you want to speak to someone at the other end of your street, or in a different town or country, you probably use a telephone. Your telephone is linked to other telephones through the telephone network. Every telephone has its own number. When you dial the number of your friend's telephone, this links your telephone through the network to your friend's telephone.

△ Early telephones had no buttons or dials. You asked the telephone operator to connect you to the number you wanted.

1

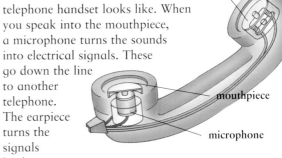

earpiece

mouthpiece

microphone

▷ This is what the inside of a telephone handset looks like. When you speak into the mouthpiece, a microphone turns the sounds into electrical signals. These go down the line to another telephone. The earpiece turns the signals back into sound.

△ **1** You can make a simple telephone with two empty yogurt containers and some string. Ask an adult to make a small hole in the base of each container.

2

Fact box

• The telephone was invented in America in 1876 by Alexander Graham Bell, a Scottish engineer and teacher.

▷ **2** Push one end of the string into one of the holes. Tie a knot to stop it slipping out. Do the same thing with the other container. Make sure the knots are tight.

one person holds a container over their ear

▷ A telephone is linked to an exchange. Exchanges are connected to each other, by cables, radio, and sometimes by satellite links. All these things make up the telephone network.

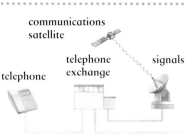

communications satellite

telephone exchange   signals   telephone exchange

telephone

telephone

△ A fax machine plugs into a telephone line, just like an ordinary telephone. It has a scanner that turns words and pictures into electrical signals. The fax sends these to another fax machine.

△ The telephones that we use at home are linked to the local exchange by wires. Signals go along these as pulses of electricity. Some telephone cables are made of thin glass fibers called optical fibers. Signals travel along these as flashes of light.

the other person talks into a container

3

the string must be pulled tight

△ The other fax machine turns the signals back into words and pictures. It prints them onto paper.

◁ 3 Vibrations made by your voice travel along the string. They make the other pot vibrate. Your friend hears these vibrations as your voice.

Find out more
Electricity
Inventions and Discoveries
Satellites
Sound

Television

What sort of television programs do you like best? To make a televison program, a camera has to take pictures. These go from the camera to a television station, and on to a transmitter. This sends them to your television set, along wires or on radio waves. Satellite television programs travel on microwaves.

△ The pictures on these screens are from security cameras. A guard watches for intruders. A system like this is called closed circuit television.

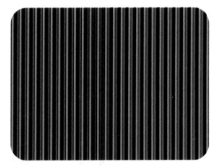

△ This is a magnified close-up of a television screen. You can see bands of red, green, and blue. All television pictures are made up of just these three colors.

△ This camera is recording a sports event. The camera operator sees the picture the camera is taking on a small television screen.

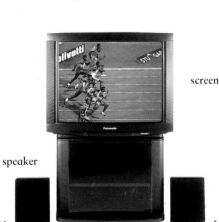

screen

speaker

◁ A television set turns signals from the television station into the pictures you see on the screen. It plays sound through the loudspeakers.

Find out more
Color
Electricity
Light
Microwaves
Radio
Video

Universe

The Universe is made up of everything that exists. It includes the Earth and everything on it, the Moon and the planets, the Sun, and billions of other stars. Scientists believe that the Universe was created billions of years ago, with a huge explosion. They call this the Big Bang. It scattered gas which formed the stars, galaxies, and planets—including Earth.

▽ Stars cannot shine forever. After billions of years, they fade and die. Some dying stars grow huge and red and then explode. The explosion in the top corner of this picture is called a supernova.

◁ Stars are not evenly spread out in the Universe. They are clumped together in enormous groups called galaxies. There are billions of galaxies. Some are blobs, some are round, and some are spiral-shaped.

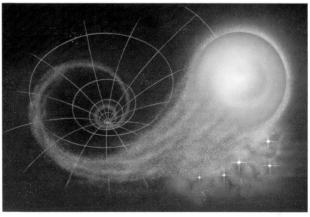

△ Our Solar System is part of a spiral-shaped galaxy called the Milky Way. All the stars you see at night are in the Milky Way.

△ Astronomers have found some very strange things in outer space. A black hole is a part of space where gravity is so strong that light cannot escape from it. This picture shows dust and gas being pulled into a black hole.

Long ago, people named the groups of stars in the sky after gods, people, and animals. We call these groups constellations.

◁△ These two constellations are called Scorpio, the scorpion (left), and Leo, the lion (above).

▽ This constellation is the Great Bear. It is also called the Plough or Big Dipper. Can you work out why?

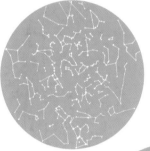

◁ Study a star map. Then, on a clear night, see which constellations and stars you can spot in the sky.

northern hemisphere

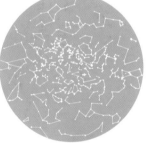

southern hemisphere

△ This is a constellation you will only see from Australia and other countries in the southern hemisphere. People call it the Southern Cross because the stars in it form the shape of a cross.

▷ There is a giant telescope inside this dome. It is high up on a mountainside. Because it is above the clouds, the sky is clear, and astronomers can get a good view of the stars and planets.

Find out more
Day and Night
Solar System
Space travel

Video

Video is a way of recording moving pictures. The recording is done on videotape. This is like the tape used in a music cassette. With a video camera, you can record your own moving pictures and play them on television, using a videocassette recorder (VCR).

▽ A camcorder is a video camera and recorder all in one. You look through the viewfinder to see what you are recording.

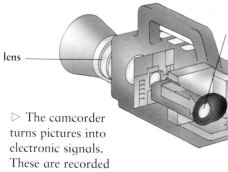

lens

viewfinder

▷ The camcorder turns pictures into electronic signals. These are recorded on the video tape.

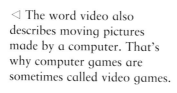

◁ A VCR is used to record television programs for watching later. It can also play prerecorded video tapes, such as films and cartoons.

◁ The word video also describes moving pictures made by a computer. That's why computer games are sometimes called video games.

Find out more
Camera
Electricity
Recording
Television

Volcano

Under the Earth's hard crust lies hot, molten rock called magma. Sometimes pressure builds up under the Earth and pushes the magma up through cracks in the crust. This is how a volcano erupts. When it reaches the surface, the magma is known as lava. Some volcanoes erupt with a bang and shoot gas, dust, and lava into the air.

△ These huge fountains of hot water and steam are called geysers. They are often found near volcanoes. Water is heated by the hot rocks under the ground and gushes to the surface through cracks in the Earth's crust.

△ **1** Make a model volcano. Put about two teaspoons of bicarbonate of soda into a spice jar. Build a clay model of a volcano around the jar.

△ **2** Pour 3.5 fluid ounces of vinegar into the jar and watch your volcano erupt. To make colored lava, add food coloring to the vinegar.

▽ When a volcano erupts, molten rock flows along underground channels and then pours out of the top of the volcano. As the lava cools, it forms a cone-shaped mountain.

△ The hole at the top of a volcano is called the crater. In some volcanoes, smoke rises from the crater all the time.

Find out more
Earth
Energy
Fuels
Melting and Boiling

Water

Water is the most common liquid on Earth. Most of it lies in the oceans. These cover two-thirds of the Earth. There is also water in rivers and lakes, and in the air. There is water trapped as ice in the Arctic and Antarctic. Even you are mostly water. It makes up two-thirds of your body. All living things need water to stay alive.

△ 1 Find out what happens when water freezes. Fill a plastic bottle with water. Do not put the top on it. Put the bottle in the freezer.

How water gets to our homes

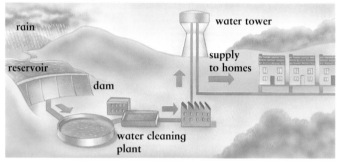

rain

water tower

reservoir

supply to homes

dam

water cleaning plant

△ How do you get water for washing and drinking? It probably comes out of a faucet. This water is stored in reservoirs, often far away. Then, underground pipes carry it to your home.

△ 2 As the water freezes, ice comes out of the bottle's neck. This is because water gets bigger when it freezes. Most liquids get smaller.

▷ Seawater is warmed by the Sun and evaporates. When it cools, it forms rain clouds. Streams and rivers carry the rain to the sea. This is called the water cycle.

The water cycle

water evaporates (becomes the gas, water vapor)

clouds form

rainwater flows from the land into streams and rivers

△ Water can wear away a river's banks and bed. This is called erosion. The Grand Canyon was made by erosion. It took millions of years for the Colorado River to wear the canyon away.

▽ An iceberg is a giant lump of ice. It floats in the sea because ice is lighter than water. Only a tiny part of it shows above the surface. Most of it is underwater. Icebergs form from the huge icefields in the coldest parts of the world, or from rivers of ice called glaciers. Pieces of ice break off and float away into the sea.

△ **1** Try this experiment to see why putting salt on roads stops them from getting icy. Stir salt into a jug of water until no more will dissolve. Pour the salty water into a dish. Fill another dish with plain water.

△ **2** Put both dishes in the freezer. The salty water takes longer to freeze because it freezes at a lower temperature than plain water. So salting wet roads means it must get much colder before ice forms.

Find out more
Air and
Atmosphere
Gases
Hot and Cold
Liquids
Melting and
Boiling
Solids
Waves

Waves

There are many different kinds of waves, but the ones you know best are the ones in the sea. When waves travel across the sea, they do not carry any water with them. The water just moves up and down as the waves pass through it. Waves at sea are caused by the wind blowing across the surface. Light, sound, and radio signals also travel in waves.

△ **1** See how waves spread across water. Fill a plastic bowl with water. Wait for the surface to become flat and calm. Drop a marble or a small stone into the middle of the bowl.

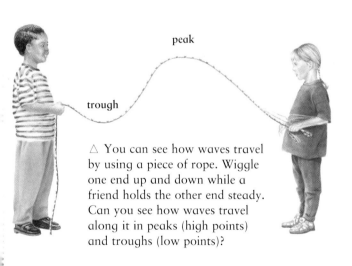

peak

trough

△ You can see how waves travel by using a piece of rope. Wiggle one end up and down while a friend holds the other end steady. Can you see how waves travel along it in peaks (high points) and troughs (low points)?

△ **2** Did you see the waves spread out in rings? Did you see the waves bounce back from the sides of the bowl?

◁ When waves reach the seashore, they bunch up together and get steeper and steeper. When they reach the beach, they fall over.

Find out more
Microwaves
Radio
Sound
Television
Water

Weather

What is the weather like today where you live? Is it sunny or cloudy? Is it windy and raining? The different kinds of weather are caused by the way the Sun, atmosphere, and spinning Earth all work together. The kind of weather a place has throughout the year is called its climate.

▽ 1 Do you know how clouds form? Try this experiment to find out. Put some warm water in a large jar. You cannot see it, but water vapor will rise from the water. Cover the jar with a metal tray full of ice cubes.

△ 2 The water vapor meets cold air near the tray. It turns into millions of tiny water droplets. Clouds are also made from tiny droplets that form when water vapor cools.

△ Different places have different kinds of weather. The place in this picture has very warm weather all year long. We say it has a tropical climate. Places that have warm summers and cool winters have a temperate climate. Places that are cold all year long have a polar climate.

▷ Satellites in space take pictures of the Earth. These show weather forecasters the way that clouds and storms are moving. The forecasters use these to work out what the weather will be like for the next few days.

▽ In many tropical countries, there is heavy rain for several months of the year. Farmers depend on this rain to make their crops grow.

△ Storms often bring very strong winds and heavy rain. They can cause great damage to homes and farmers' fields. The wind can blow down trees and tear roofs from buildings. At sea, it can cause huge waves. Floodwater can wash away trees and even homes.

▷ A tornado is a swirling column of fast-moving air. It races along, sucking up anything in its path.

▽ Clouds come in different shapes and sizes. Each gives a clue about the sort of weather that is coming. For example, cumulus clouds mean heavy rain is on the way.

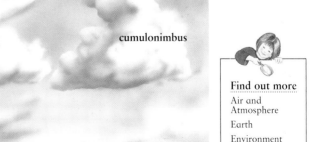

cirrus

cumulonimbus

cumulus

stratus

Find out more
Air and Atmosphere
Earth
Environment
Water

X rays

X rays are waves, similar to microwaves and light waves. They can pass right through flesh, but not through bones. X-ray photographs are used in hospitals, for example, to see if bones are broken. The bones show up light on a dark background.

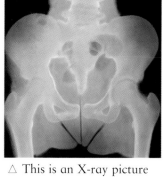

△ This is an X-ray picture of part of a child's back. It was taken to see if any bones were broken.

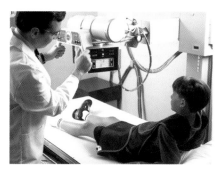

▷ This X-ray machine is being prepared to fire X rays down through the patient's leg. The X rays hit a sheet of film on the table beneath.

▽ X rays are used at airports to check people's baggage for dangerous items. As the bags go through the machine, the screen shows what is inside them.

One or two X rays will not harm you. Too many can be dangerous. People who work with them go behind a protective screen while the X rays are being taken.

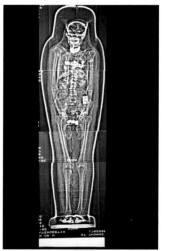

◁ In ancient Egypt, people wrapped dead bodies in cloth to preserve them. These bandaged bodies are called mummies. Modern scientists can use X rays to look inside the wrappings.

Find out more
Atoms
Microwaves
Nuclear energy
Radio
Universe

Z

▷ Zodiac

The twelve signs of the Zodiac are named after constellations (groups of stars). They are sometimes called star signs. Astrologers are people who believe that your star sign, and the movement of the Moon and the other planets, affect what happens in your life.

Aries   Taurus   Gemini

Cancer   Leo   Virgo

Libra   Scorpio   Sagittarius

Capricorn   Aquarius   Pisces

▷ Zero

The number zero means none. It is very important in mathematics to have a symbol for none. Imagine trying to work out problems without it. Zero was invented in India about 1,000 years ago. Arab traders learned about it and passed it on to people in Europe.

▽ Zipper

A zipper is a type of fastener for clothes and other things. A zipper has rows of tiny plastic or metal teeth on each edge. When you do up a zipper, the teeth lock together. When you undo it, they come apart.

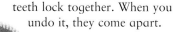

△ Zoology

Zoology is a part of the science of biology. People who study it are called zoologists. They study the way animals live and behave.

> **Find out more**
> Inventions and Discoveries
> Living things
> Numbers
> Universe

Glossary

A **glossary** is a list of useful words. Some of the words used in this book may be new to you. You can find out more about them here.

astronomer a person who studies the Solar System and the Universe.

atmosphere the thick blanket of air that surrounds the whole Earth.

atom a tiny particle of matter. Everything around you is made of atoms joined together.

battery a store of electricity. When a battery is connected to an electric circuit, the electricity flows out of the battery and around the circuit.

billion one thousand million (1,000,000,000).

bulb a glass globe that gives off light when an electric current flows through it.

carbon dioxide a gas found in the Earth's atmosphere. Plants use carbon dioxide to make their food.

cell one of the tiny building blocks that make up the body of an animal or plant.

center of gravity the point on an object where the object's weight is evenly balanced. The center of gravity of a disk is in the middle of the disk. Your center of gravity is near your belly button.

coal a hard, shiny, black substance found under the ground. It is used as a fuel.

cog a wheel with teeth around the outside. Two cogs placed with their teeth touching can turn each other around.

cosmic rays particles and waves that come from stars and other objects in space.

crater a large hole on the surface of a planet. Craters are made by crashing meteors or volcanoes.

crust the hard outer skin of a planet.

cursor pointer on a computer screen. For example, when you type on a computer, a cursor shows you where the letters you type will appear on the screen.

density how much a certain volume of a substance weighs. For example, water has a much higher density than air because it weighs more.

diesel a liquid fuel made from oil that is found under the ground and seas.

digital anything that is made up of numbers.

earthquake when the ground shakes and cracks because of rocks moving under the ground.

echo when a sound you hear once bounces off a hard surface so that you can hear it again.

elastic anything that goes back into shape after it has been stretched or squashed.

electric current a stream of tiny particles (called electrons) moving along a wire.

electromagnet a magnet made when an electric current passes through a coil of wire.

electronics electric circuits that control machines, such as computers, electronic watches, and washing machines. Most electronic circuits are very tiny.

erosion when soil and rocks are gradually worn away by wind, water, ice, or waves.

film a thin sheet of plastic covered in chemicals that change when light or x rays hit them to record a picture.

force a push or a pull.

germs tiny bugs that can cause illnesses if they get into your body.

hemisphere one half of the Earth. The Earth is divided into the northern hemisphere (above the equator) and the southern hemisphere (below the equator).

image the picture made by a lens or mirror when it bends light.

intruder a person in a building who is not supposed to be there.

loudspeaker a device that turns an electric current into sound.

microscope a device that uses lenses to make tiny objects look much bigger.

molecule a group of atoms joined together. Some molecules have just a few atoms. Others molecules have thousands of atoms.

molten a solid that has melted. The word molten is normally used for things that have to be very hot before they melt, such as rocks and metals.

nectar a sugary liquid that is made in the flowers of some plants. Bees use the nectar to make honey.

nocturnal an animal that sleeps during the day and hunts for food at night.

nucleus the central part of an atom.

orbit the path that a satellite takes when it is circling around a planet or a star.

oxygen a gas found in the Earth's atmosphere. All animals need to breathe oxygen to live. Oxygen is also needed for burning.

pollution waste material in the environment, such as poisonous gases, chemicals from factories, and garbage.

polyethylene a type of plastic. Most plastic bags, like the ones you get in a supermarket, are made from polyethylene.

primary colors a set of colors that all other colors are made from.

robot a machine that can be programmed to do many different jobs.

seedling a new plant that has just started growing from a seed.

skeleton a frame that supports an animal. You have a skeleton of bones inside your body.

steel a type of metal made from the metal iron with some carbon added to it.

stem the part of a plant that sticks up from the ground and supports the rest of the plant.

telescope a device that uses lenses or mirrors to make far-off objects look much closer.

tides when the level of the sea goes up and down, normally twice a day.

transmitter an aerial that sends out radio signals.

volume the amount of space that an object takes up.

water vapor the gas made when water boils. It is the gas form of water.

weight the pull of gravity on an object. Everything on Earth has weight.

Index

This index helps you find subjects in the book. It is in alphabetical order. Main entries are in **dark**, or **bold**, type.